CHANGING PATTERNS
IN
FOREIGN LANGUAGE PROGRAMS

NEWBURY HOUSE SERIES:

INNOVATIONS IN FOREIGN LANGUAGE EDUCATION

HOWARD B. ALTMAN, Series Editor

Published:

INDIVIDUALIZING FOREIGN LANGUAGE INSTRUCTION:
Proceedings of the Stanford Conference
Edited by HOWARD B. ALTMAN and ROBERT L. POLITZER

INDIVIDUALIZING THE FOREIGN LANGUAGE CLASSROOM:
Perspectives for Teachers
Edited by HOWARD B. ALTMAN

SPEAKING IN MANY TONGUES:
Essays in Foreign-Language Teaching
WILGA M. RIVERS

CHANGING PATTERNS IN FOREIGN LANGUAGE PROGRAMS:
Report of the Illinois Conference
on Foreign Languages in Junior and Community Colleges, 1972
Edited by WILGA M. RIVERS, LOUISE H. ALLEN,
SANDRA J. SAVIGNON, and RICHARD T. SCANLAN

Forthcoming:

PERFORMING WITH OBJECTIVES
FLORENCE STEINER

INDIVIDUALIZING FOREIGN LANGUAGE LEARNING:
An Organic Process
GERALD LOGAN

THE MANAGEMENT OF FOREIGN LANGUAGE INSTRUCTION
JOHN and VALERIE BOCKMAN

DESIGNS FOR LANGUAGE TEACHER EDUCATION
ALAN GARFINKEL (Control Editor), LOLA MACKEY, BONNIE BUSSE,
GENELLE MORAIN, ROBERT MORREY, MANUEL PACHECO,
and JEAN-PIERRE BERWALD

FOREIGN LANGUAGE EDUCATION:
A Manual for Administrators
HELEN CAREY

CHANGING PATTERNS IN FOREIGN LANGUAGE PROGRAMS

*REPORT OF THE ILLINOIS CONFERENCE
ON FOREIGN LANGUAGES IN JUNIOR
AND COMMUNITY COLLEGES, 1972*

*Edited by WILGA M. RIVERS
LOUISE H. ALLEN
SANDRA J. SAVIGNON
RICHARD T. SCANLAN*

NEWBURY HOUSE PUBLISHERS, INC.

NEWBURY HOUSE PUBLISHERS, INC.

Language Science
Language Teaching
Language Learning

68 Middle Road, Rowley, Massachusetts 01969

Library of Congress Card Number: 72-93484
ISBN: 912066-17-2

Cover design by Holly Nichols

Printed in the U.S.A.   *First printing: October, 1972*

Report of the Illinois Conference on
Foreign Languages in Junior and
Community Colleges, 1972

Edited by Wilga M. Rivers
Louise H. Allen
Sandra J. Savignon
Richard T. Scanlan

TABLE OF CONTENTS

v

ACKNOWLEDGEMENTS

The editors of this report wish to thank sincerely the Communications Division and the Office of Community Information at Parkland College, Champaign, and the Departments of Classics, French, German, Linguistics, Slavic Languages and Literatures, Spanish, and the Center for East European Studies at the University of Illinois at Urbana-Champaign for their financial and material support which made the Illinois Conference on Foreign Languages in Junior and Community Colleges and this report possible, and the Department of English as a Second Language and the Center for Asian Studies at the University of Illinois for their assistance in the planning stages. We also wish to thank President William M. Staerkel of Parkland College and Dean Robert W. Rogers of the College of Liberal Arts and Sciences and Professor Ernest Anderson, Coordinator of University-Junior College Relations, at the University of Illinois for their personal interest in our project. The conference itself would never have been realized were it not for the devoted work of Professor Vincent Dell'Orto of the Department of German of the University of Illinois in the material organization of the Conference, and of Miss Paulette Pelc as secretarial assistant for the regional and state conferences and the assembling of the report. We are also indebted to Miss Judith Jones and Mrs. Clara Lindsey for their competent preparation of the final script and to Mrs. Harriet Hatchell for cheerful support in many material details at all stages of the project. To our regional representatives and all in our own departments who encouraged and helped us we express our appreciation and gratitude.

Proceeds from the sale of this book will be divided between the Communications Division at Parkland College, Champaign, and the Unit for Foreign language Studies and Research at the University of Illinois, Urbana, Illinois.

Wilga M. Rivers
Louise H. Allen
Sandra J. Savignon
Richard T. Scanlan

Urbana-Champaign, Illinois
June, 1972

SECTION I:

THE JUNIOR - COMMUNITY COLLEGE

1. FOREIGN LANGUAGE INSTRUCTION: A MANDATE FOR PLURALISM

HOWARD B. ALTMAN
University of Washington

The growth of the community college movement
in the United States has been acclaimed as
perhaps the most significant development in
education in the past half century.[1] The
first two-year college opened its doors in
Joliet, Illinois in 1902, and today new community colleges are opening doors around the
nation at the rate of almost one per week.
Whether the community college will provide
pedagogically viable and exciting alternatives for the majority of high school graduates, as Cosand postulates in *Campus 1980*,
or whether it will succumb to vast internal
and external pressures for perpetuating academic status quo, as Jencks and Riesman fear
in *The Academic Revolution*, the future of the
community college is macrocosm may well parallel developments within the microcosm of our
own sphere of conern at this conference:
foreign language education.

3

When a distinguished working committee
at the 1970 Northeast Conference on the
Teaching of Foreign Languages concluded that
"second-language learning should be an integral part of the basic education of every
child," the committee specified that instruction must be geared to the interests and
abilities of a diverse population of learners.[4] This notion of heterogeneity in learning styles and objectives, of diverse short-
and long-term goals, of various levels of
experience and commitment is the hallmark of
the community college par excellence. It is
this very diversity in the backgrounds of its
clientele which forces the community college
to respond to pressures quite alien in most
four-year institutions, whose student population frequently has more homogeneous and
traditional reasons for attendance. The
September 1971 Student Personnel Handbook of
Parkland College, Champaign, for example,
lists some thirteen types of students who are
enrolled at the college. Let me quote from
this list:

1) The high school graduate of moderate
   ability and achievement who enters
   junior college right after high school
   as a full-time student with the inten-
   tion of transferring to a given institution with a particular major.
2) The high school graduate of special
   aptitude and achievement who seeks
   rapid training for early employment.
3) The low achiever in high school who
   finally awakens to the values of college and then becomes highly motivated
   to enroll in a junior college transfer
   program for which he is not equipped,
   yet who may have the necessary potential.
4) The able high school graduate who
   could go to any college but selects

4

the local community college because of
the respect and loyalty he has gained
for it or for reasons of convenience.
5) The high school graduate of low ability who enters junior college because
of social pressures or because he can
not find employment.
6) The students of varying ability and
ages but with high valuation of the
world of ideas who primarily seek intellectual stimulation.
7) The very bright high school graduate,
eligible for admission to a major
university, who may lack the necessary
social maturity and intellectual dis-
position.
8) The intellectually capable but unmo-
tivated, disinterested high school
graduate who comes to junior college
to explore, hoping it will offer him
something, but he does not know what.
9) The transfer from a four-year college
who either failed or withdrew after an
unsatisfactory experience.
10) The high school dropout, perhaps from
a minority group and a culturally dis-
advantaged family, with only grade-
school-level skills and a strong interest in securing vocational training.
11) The youngsters and also adults who
fully believe the societal direction
that the road to success leads through
a college campus but whose perception
of success is so murky that its relationship to learning is virtually
lost.
12) The immature high school graduate
whose current concept of college has
never extended much beyond girls
(boys), ballgames, rallies, and
dances.

13) The adult who was employed, or in the
    military service, or in the home for
    a number of years, and who now is
    motivated to pursue an associate and
    perhaps a baccalaureate degree, how-
    ever long it may take.[5]

It is obvious from the above descriptions
that students at Parkland College, as at so
many two-year institutions throughout the
nation, represent a host of different age
groups, cultural backgrounds, levels of ability, attitudes and motivation toward learning,
and career aspirations. In a recent study of
the community college, Blocker, Plummer, and
Richardson point out that, although national-
ly the majority of incoming freshmen aspire
to complete a bachelor's degree at a four-
year institution, in fact no more than one-
third of them ever go beyond their sophmore
year.[6] Stated in different terms, although
at Parkland College, for example, some fifty
per cent of the student body aspires to complete at least a baccalaureate, the "preparation for transfer" function of two-year institutions in the development of the curriculum may have been sorely overrated. Statistics tend to support this. At Parkland as
at most community colleges, the majority of
students use the college as a means to obtain
specific and limited objectives. Some ninety
per cent of Parkland's students classify vocationally related goals as essential or
important to them.[7]

How is the foreign language program at a
community college to respond to the variety
of goals and the gamut of abilities which
characterize its clientele? One thing is
certain: if the foreign language program in
the two-year institution is designed solely
to duplicate course offerings in the local or
state college or university's lower division,

6

it is poorly and inadequately providing for
the needs, abilities, and interests of as
many as two-thirds of its student body.

There is no more certain road to failure
in the 1970's, it seems to me, than for the
community college foreign language program to
be allowed to become a carbon copy of the
first two years of the four-year institution's
curriculum. The "preparation for transfer"
argument is not valid, not only from the
point of view of number of students affected,
but also on the basis of a requirement for
transfer passed down from on high. It is uncertain for how much longer colleges and
universities will maintain entrance requirements in foreign language in their present
form. We have already witnessed the weaken-
ing or removal of graduation requirements at
many four-year institutions. If the community college fashions its foreign language
course offerings solely upon the presence of
a requirement that transfer students offer a
certain number of credit hours in "academically oriented" foreign language instruction,
the foreign language department may soon find
itself facing empty classrooms in even greater numbers than today. Already in the state
of Washington, where the transfer requirement is two academic quarters of foreign language study, there are frequently so few
students who exceed the required amount that
in many two-year institutions intermediate-
level instruction is either no longer offered for credit or offered only if faculty members will take on such students as an "over-
load."

The question of maintaining "academic
standards"--the so-called "college-grade
shibboleth," as Cosand has termed it, is and
probably has been for some time the greatest

7

obstacle to successful foreign language programs at the community college level.[8] It is
ironic that the community college, whose educational mission is to provide opportunity
for higher education and vocational training
to all qualified members of the community,
should operate in such a way that it caters
only to the needs of the "academically tal-
ented" or "academically inclined" as if the
only reason to study a foreign language at
the community college level were to be able
to take advanced courses as a transfer student at a four-year institution. The community college's "open door policy" has become,
at least in foreign language education, a
"swinging door, gently--or not so gently--
pushing out the unwanted student."[9]

If foreign language instruction is to
survive and prosper in the two-year college,
efforts must be made to provide options for
all students to attain goals in foreign language study *of personal value to them*. In
other words, foreign language teachers at
the two-year college are faced with a mandate
for pluralism in the curriculum. The presence of diverse student abilities and interests dictates a multiplicity of foreign language experiences. The "academically-orient-
ed" lower division course need not disappear;
some students--indeed, many at some institu-
tions--will select this option. But for the
majority of students whose formal education
will never exceed an associate of arts degree, there is a manifest need for new curricula, if community college foreign language
teachers wish to provide viable educational
experiences for a sizable percentage of the
college's population.

How is this to be done? What would these
other "options" look like? Wouldn't the
"quality" of the course be diminished if stu-

8

dents are allowed to pursue different goals?
As a first step, foreign language teachers
might poll their students as to their goals
in foreign language study. The results
would probably prove surprising. Some students, especially among the adults in evening
classes, are desirous of learning enough
French or Spanish or German to get along overseas next summer with minimum difficulty.
They need a narrow range of training, for
their basic goal is survival in a foreign
land and language, not Cultural ("capital C")
appreciation, not syntactic refinement, not
exercise in drawing accent marks. (Incidentally, the failure of the community college
to respond to this need of an ever-increasing
number of travelers has resulted in a land-
office business for Berlitz and the other
"language schools," for whom the customer is
always right.) Other students may plan to
take a position in a specific trade overseas.
They need to become familiar with a specialized lexicon. Still other students may be
interested in *Reading Scientific German,
Italian for Opera Lovers, French for Chefs* or
Spanish for Social Workers. The two-year institution is uniquely constituted to develop
"mini-courses" along such lines. As Jakobovits has pointed out, such courses are likely
to transform the "student motivation" problem
into an overcrowded classroom problem.[10]

But pluralism means more than designing
"mini-courses" to meet certain needs. It im-
plies a recognition of the fact that students
at a community college have different ethnic,
linguistic, cultural, and socioeconomic backgrounds, and that provision for these differences must be made in the construction of the
curriculum. Blocker, Plummer, and Richardson
have suggested that students at the two-year
institution tend to come from socioeconomic
groups whose values are not congruent with

9

those of middle- and upper-middle-class faculty members and administrators.[11] Think back,
if you will, to the humorous yet frustrating
consequences of the clash in values between
Hyman Kaplan and his English instructor, in
Leonard Q. Ross' classic *The Education of
Hyman Kaplan*.[12]

One of the chief sources of difficulty
which community college foreign language
teachers in the state of Washington have pin-
pointed is the lack of articulation with local high school programs. I am sure that
this difficulty is not indigenous to Washington alone. One solution to this problem is
to provide for the continuous progress of
students within the "academically oriented"
track. In a continuous progress program, an
incoming student may enter the study of a
foreign language at any point in the curriculum (determined by diagnostic tests), and at
any point in the academic year. This means
that students are allowed to proceed through
their curriculum materials at their own pace.
There ceases to be a problem in coordination
of systems when incoming students can choose
a course of studies corresponding to their
needs and interests, and can pursue their
studies at a pace congruent with their abilities. It is really not that difficult to
transform the "fearsome foreign language
hour," as Moskowitz has termed it,[13] into a
fun-filled and profitable one, for *all* students.

Such attempts at individualizing instruction at the community college level by providing options in the curriculum and by allowing each learner to work at his own pace can
succeed only if individualizaion is accompanied by humanization. It behooves the teacher
to adopt a new attitude toward both his discipline and his students. The mandate for

10

pluralism must extend to the affective domain
as well. The foreign language teacher must
accept and believe in the value of language
study for conceivably as many different purposes as there are students in the program.
He must emotionally support the student who
wishes merely to dabble in foreign language
study as sincerely as he supports a narcissis-
tically-viewed disciple. He must accept the
notion that foreign language study can be
meaningful in *any* amount, and that the determination of meaningfulness can only be made
by the learner, not by the teacher. Thus,
the student whose sole purpose in foreign language study is to acquire enough vocabulary
to avoid being exploited on his trip to
Europe next summer is as legitimate an object
for the teacher's concern and attention as
the prospective foreign language major.

The teacher must also adopt a new attitude
toward the learning process. He must recognize that very little indeed is currently
known about how individuals learn foreign languages, or anything else in the community
college curriculum. An attitude of pluralism
means an acceptance of the fact that different students learn in different ways, at different times, by different means, for different purposes. These differences imply that
no one "method" of teaching foreign languages
will ever be "best" for all students. They
also imply that the emphasis in the 1970s
must shift from language-*teaching* to language-
learning, and to the ways in which teachers
can facilitate the learning of foreign languages.

The comprehensive community college was
created to offer the opportunity for personal
betterment to every learner in the community,
from seventeen to seventy and beyond. Its
foreign language program must reflect this

11

spirit of optimism in its curricular offerings and in its philosophy of instruction.
The reasons for studying foreign languages
today are as valid as they have ever been,
and the advantages of knowing a second language in the jet age are solidly supported.
If our school and college enrollments have
been decreasing in recent years, we might
ponder the fact that the enrollment in private language schools such as Berlitz has not
fallen, and in fact, until the recent economic depression in this country, had been increasing at the rate of fifteen percent per
year--despite the fact that foreign language
instruction is either free or quite inexpensive in *our* classrooms, and often quite costly in the private language schools. When the
foreign language learner prefers to pay dear-
ly for something that we have been offering
him free, this should tell us something. The
1970s may be our last chance to do something
about it.

NOTES

1. Clyde E. Blocker, Robert H. Plummer, and
    Richard C. Richardson, Jr., *The Two-Year
    College: A Social Synthesis* (Englewood
    Cliffs, New Jersey: Prentice-Hall, 1965),
    p.1.
2. Joseph P. Cosand, "The Community College
    in 1980," in Alvin C. Eurich, ed. *Campus
    1980: The Shape of the Future in Ameri-
    can Higher Education* (New York: Dell
    Publishing Co., 1968),pp.134-48.
3. Christopher Jencks and David Riesman,
    The Academic Revolution (New York:
    Doubleday & Co., 1968),pp.481-92.
4. Eleanor L. Sandstrom and Paul Pimsleur,
    co-eds., "Foreign Languages for All
    Students" in Joseph A. Tursi, ed. *Foreign
    Languages and the 'New' Student.* Reports
    of the Working Committees, Northeast Con-

ference on the Teaching of Foreign Languages (New York: MLA-ACTFL Materials
Center, 1970),pp.105-33.

5. *Parkland College Student Personnel Handbook,* September, 1971,pp.14-14. My
appreciation to Professor Wilga M. Rivers
of the University of Illinois for supplying me with a copy of this material.

6. Blocker, Plummer, and Richardson, p.121.

7. *Parkland College Student Personnel Handbook,* p.15.

8. Cosand, p.141.

9. Cosand, p.141.

10. Leon A. Jakobovits, *Foreign Language
Learning: A Psycholinguistic Analysis
of the Issues* (Rowley, Massachusetts:
Newbury House Publishers, 1970),p.144.

11. Blocker, Plummer, and Richardson,
pp.130-1.

12. Leonard Q. Ross, *The Education of Hyman
Kaplan* (New York: Harcourt, Brace, 1937).

13. Gertrude Moskowitz, "The Fearsome Foreign
Language Hour," *French Review* XXXVIII,
No. 6,1965,pp.781-86.

2. THE COLLEGES OF THE 80's — OR WHERE THE ACTION IS

LOUISE H. ALLEN
Parkland College, Champaign, Illinois

Our topic, *The Colleges of the 80's*, is a
term frequently applied to comprehensive two-
year community colleges as they have developed in recent years across the country. The
reason for the label is that many educational
theorists think "the community college...
will, by 1980, have accepted virtually the
entire responsibility for providing the first
two years of college work."[1] It will be a
true center of learning, providing educational opportunities for both youths and adults,
day and night, twelve months a year.[2] Since
at this time we are still trying to survive
the Swinging, Scintillating and (on a lot of
campuses) Starveling 70's, may I suggest an
alternative sobriquet for now--the Colleges
Where the Action Is.

What are these strange, new (at least to
us here in the Midwest) critters, the fast-
est growing animals in academe? One authority says,

> The community junior college is the
> most recent addition to this family
> of post-high-school educational in-
> stitutions [including two-year lib-
> eral arts colleges, technical insti-
> tutions, trade schools, etc.]. As
> yet, it has failed to achieve from
> its elders full understanding or com-
> plete cooperation. Part of this fail-
> ure derives from the multiplicity of
> its functions. The community junior
> college does indeed offer two years
> of conventional higher education to
> some of its students. Yet it is not
> only a lower division. It adds to
> the college transfer curriculums
> other courses adapted to the 'mental
> capacity and educational level' of
> its students[3]

and we might add, to the needs of its home
community.

The community college *is* comprehensive,
and it is community-oriented. It looks very
different from town to town, and even from
neighborhood to neighborhood of a metropolis
like New York or Chicago. But basically it
has the following features.

1) It is a *student-centered* institution,
attracting at least two kinds of students
who have not previously been drawn to traditional colleges or universities--namely,
those who cannot or do not care to devote full
time to study.

2) It is a *teaching* institution.

3) It is *easily accessible* physically to

15

people in its district, and it is *relatively
inexpensive* to attend.

It has at least four identifiable functions, each with a bearing on the teaching
of foreign languages within its walls (or behind its storefronts, as the case often is
these days).

1) It is the place where many students
begin what will be a baccalaureate or even
a graduate program eventually. This is the
transfer function, the one in which foreign
languages are most likely at this time to
bulk large, giving students the opportunity
to satisfy senior institutions' language requirements before transfer.

2) It offers *career* or vocational-technical programs, usually terminal in nature and
one or two years in length. Foreign languages may be directly important here, in
preparing bilingual secretaries, policemen,
or community service workers, for example.
Also, the foreign language staff is often
involved in the design and teaching of a
course in the humanities or in current social
problems for career students; the objective
of such courses is to help career students
become better citizens as well as better
workers.

3) It has a *continuing education* function,
serving adults who have full-time work responsibilities and other part-time students.
Most community colleges teach some of their
foreign languages in the continuing education
program, that is evenings and Saturdays.

4) It has a *community service* function.
Foreign languages may be involved here in the
form of non-credit courses for people expect-

16

ing to travel, or for community groups wanting to deepen their knowledge and appreciation of a non-American language and culture, or in sponsering foreign film series, folk dance festivals, travel lectures and the like. The non-credit courses often differ radically from the conventional transfer course, having some of the features of a travelogue, some resemblance to a Berlitz-type crash course in useful phrases, and some homely tips on getting along in a foreign country; or concentrating on aspects of the literature or culture not usually treated in university courses such as "pop" novels and street slang. On my own campus, which is presently one of the many storefront ones, the foreign language faculty turns window dresser once a year, putting together a display of *realia* for the general public to view, as advertising for our free foreign film festival.

Now what do I, as a chairman in this complex kind of instruction, look for in selecting candidates for FL jobs? What kind of person do I think can fill our needs in all these areas? The person who has most or all of the following attributes.

1) A thorough, native or near-native command of the language, and personal knowledge of its contemporary culture.

2) What I call flexibility, versatility and personality--with a generous salting of imagination and a talent for thinking fast on one's feet.

3) Familiarity with (and hopefully affection for) mechanical aids--language labs, films, filmstrips, slides, overhead transparencies, cassette tapes, electronic classrooms, computer-assisted instruction.

4) A real interest in, and enthusiasm for, teaching the basic courses--elementary and intermediate, that is.

5) Some know-how about learning theory and teaching strategies--where the sticky points in the course are and some techniques for easing students through them.

6) An interest in course and curriculum design.

7) Some knowledge, preferably gained at first hand, of what a community college is like.

8) The ability to imagine oneself in the place of a student whose academic and life experiences may have been very different from one's own.

9) And, most importantly, a genuine interest in and concern for people--all kinds of people, not just the "great reader," or the student of "culture," or the gifted future language major.

Why do I look for these particular attributes? Because I think the person who has them is best equipped to meet the concerns of the FL teacher in the community college. Number one of these concerns, I suppose, is the *heterogeneity* of both the mission of the institution and of the student body. Community college students come in all sizes, shapes and ages, and from many kinds of backgrounds. Admission is generally granted to any graduate of any high school and, in some circumstances, to anyone 18 years of age or over, regardless of previous education. The *Parkland College Student Personnel Handbook* lists 13 different types of students who come to us, ranging from the "high school dropout,"

through "the very bright high school student
...who may lack...social maturity," to "the
adult...who is now motivated to pursue a...
degree, however long it may take."[4] In an
intermediate Spanish class last year, I had
a lady who was a *magna cum laude* graduate in
1935 of one of the fine women's colleges on
the East Coast; she sat side-by-side in the
classroom with students who had just graduated in the lowest quartile of their classes
from our local district's high schools.

[Our college, incidentally, serves 26
high school districts, and even within the
"routine" high school graduate group there is
wide divergence: about half of our students
have graduated in high school classes of
around 400, the other half in classes of less
tha 100. Some are widely traveled; some feel
that in coming to Champaign-Urbana they are
coming to the Big City. Some are just out
of high school; many have been out of school
for several years. Better than 10% of our
student body are Vietnam veterans, for instance; and many are housewives returning to
school when the last child enters kindergarten..]

This is one aspect of the heterogeneous
nature of the community college student body.
Another is in *motivation*. Some students simply want transfer credit. Others want to use
the language in a career. Some hope to improve their cultural backgrounds, and others
want to brighten up their personal GPA. In
a student-centered college, meeting the desires and needs and melding the backgrounds
of this kind of class requires some pretty
fancy footwork!

Another concern to the community college
foreign language teacher is the amount of
time available, or to be more precise *not*

19

available, to many of his students. Large
numbers of even full-time community college
students have part-time jobs. We have a few
students in our institution who are carrying
17 or 18 hour loads and working 40 or more
hours per week. It is quite usual for a student taking a 17 or 18 hour program to work
15 to 20, or perhaps even 25 hours per week.

Generally these work-study programs are
not a matter of personal taste or an attempt
to enjoy the luxuries of life while in college; they are a matter of simple economic
necessity. Most community college students
come from families with relatively low in-
come. Studies[5] of the reasons for selection
of the community college, rather than some
other, regularly show that location (nearness
to home), and relatively low tuition cost are
prime factors influencing students' choice.
The evidence is clear that the heavy work
programs of community college students reflect
a genuine concern about finances, and therefore must be taken seriously.

Obviously, his time is at a high premium
to the student who spends 18 to 24 hours in
class (depending on his number of laboratory
hours), and 15-20 or more hours a week on a
job, and often commutes considerable dis-
tances to and from the campus. Something in
his personal schedule must be sacrificed.
Frequently what it is that gets sacrificed is
individual study time, including attendance
at the language lab. The notion that the
student can spend the classic two hours of
preparation time per hour of class time simply is not practicable in most community college situations. To the foreign language
teacher, this means that much of the routine
drill that might be assigned as homework in a
more conventional college must be done in the
classroom setting. And yet all of us, stu-

20

dents and instructors, want the class to be
kept interesting; therefore the teacher needs
to have ingenuity and an appealing personality, and an ability to utilize the techniques
and technical devices that can delight the
eye and ear, broaden the horizons, and vary
the routine.

Then there is the *pragmatism* of the community college student. He wants to be able
to use what he knows, as immediately as possible; and he has relatively little use for
abstract theory. This is why I regard a high
degree of fluency as a *sine qua non*, and why
I look for applied, as well as theoretical,
knowledge of the various modern grammars, and
for skill in breaking down complex abstrac-
tions into simple, logical steps. Often the
community college FL teacher needs to create
his own programmed presentation of some aspect of language structure. In this enterprise he may well seek help from the college
Learning Laboratory, a kind of operation beginning to show up in more and more community
colleges, including my own. Its philosophy
is well stated in a report released to our
faculty this fall: "Many students come to
college with the skills necessary to succeed.
However, some students need to improve their
learning skills. One of the functions of the
junior college is to provide students with
opportunities to increase these cognitive
and affective skills...

"It is assumed that instructors want to
provide every opportunity for students to
succeed in their classes...With this in mind
it is recommended that Parkland College develop a learning laboratory."[6] The Learning
Lab is an established part of the college,
which belongs to no course or program, but into which students in *any* course of *any* program may be referred, or may refer themselves,

21

for special help, extra review, enrichment
material, or other supplementary aids.

Here again the ingenuity and technical
skill of the instructor are challenged.
Hopefully, he will try to anticipate the
kinds of materials which should be available
to his students in the Learning Lab and to
prepare the materials so that they are ready
when the student feels the need of them.

This means that he (the instructor) must
be able to analyze his course for what learning theorists call "crisis points." Can he
identify, for instance, the place at which
the students begin to feel panicky? The
point of grammar or structure (in our business) which seems to give the most students
the greatest difficulty? Can he be sure that
his identification of these points is accurate? That he really knows *why* his students
have trouble with these points? (Does their
introduction, for example, coincide neatly
with mid-term exams in other courses? And
if that is the problem, can he bring himself
to tear up his elegant course outline, and
perhaps sacrifice the logical order of his
textbook, to deal with the problem? In
other words, can the instructor be as pragmat-
ic as his students?) And does he have a
"third ear" for picking up unexpressed or
half-expressed clues and hints from students
about their needs and problems? If he does,
I want him on my staff, and I suspect most
other community college administrators do,
too.

One side comment: I have said nothing
here about background in literature; the reason is that we have almost no opportunity to
teach it in colleges like mine. In five
years at Parkland, I have taught 9 students
beyond the intermediate level; my colleagues

22

in French and German have taught 5 between
them. Community colleges in metropolitan
areas, particularly in the East and the West
present a slightly different picture here;
they have more students who enter with two,
three or four years of high school language
study than we do. But the point is worth
noting: the person who really wants to
teach Moliere of the Golden Age or Goethe
isn't likely to be happy in a community college, nor are his students and his administrators apt to be happy with him.

Therefore, let me make a special appeal
to those of you who are chairmen of departments with graduate programs: Consider
sending us applicants whose programs include
some courses in the use of A-V equipment and
media, in learning theory, in intensive
conversational practice, and in course and
curriculum design. And, if at all possible,
a course in the junior college philosophy
and history and an internship or practice
teaching experience *in a community college*.
(There is simply no substitute for meeting
the community college student face to face,
and trying out ideas and methods on real live
classes.)

Programs of this general shape exist here
and there around the country. They're labeled Master of Arts in Teaching for Junior College or (recently) Doctor of Arts or occasionally Doctor of Education for Junior College.
Some of them have been reviewed in the *ADFL
Bulletin*.[7] All too often for my taste--and I
imagine yours--they're given in Colleges of
Education and not Departments of French or
German or Spanish. All too often they're
taught and administered by people who understand the community college but don't understand our fields very well. All too often
they're frowned on or looked down on by our

best foreign language departments as "not respectable." But it looks as though a number of bright M.A.'s and Ph.D.'s are going to be making the choice, for some years to come, between teaching in a community college and not working in their chosen fields. So shouldn't we begin to think together about producing the best community college teachers we can, rather than the best unemployed university researchers we can?

These days there are many bright, able, concerned graduate students and former graduate students, who care about people and social problems, and want to put their professional interests and skills at the service of those who need them. I say let's give those graduate students the education they need for the place where they can help the most--in the colleges of the '80's.

This will mean re-designing graduate programs in some cases, and giving M.A. and Ph.D. graduates additional coursework in others. It will mean sacrificing some of your (and my) favorite courses in periods and *genres* to courses in methods and an internship. It will mean additional emphasis on linguistics, and in linguistics courses on application, probably at the expense of theory. It will mean directing dissertations in curriculum and textbook design rather than in obscure poets and novelists. It will mean sending many graduate students (as well as juniors) for a Year Abroad, with the attendant problems of finance and supervision for them. It will mean active collaboration with colleagues across departmental and even across college lines.

But it need not--and should not--mean "cheapening the degree." I certainly hope it will not mean "tracking" graduate students--

24

the bright ones to the M.A. or Ph.D program, and the problematical ones to the M.A.T. or D.A.; or switching the student who fails the Ph.D preliminary into the D.A. program. We in the community colleges want -and need- your very brightest, most inventive, most creative master's and doctoral graduates- and our salary scales usually merit their attention.[8] So does our kind of research, which is research into people-problems - learning problems, community problems- in a word, "relevant" problems. There is, and will continue to be, challenge and excitment in the colleges of the '80's. Come see; some of you might even find you'd want to join us, too. We *do* think we're Where the Action Is.

NOTES

1. Joseph P. Cosand, "The Community College in 1980," in *Campus, 1980,* Alvin C. Eurich, ed. (New York: Dell Publishing Co., 1968), p.139.
2. *Ibid.,* p.138.
3. James W. Thorton, Jr., *The Community Junior College,* 2nd edition. (New York, London and Sydney: John Wiley & Sons, Inc., 1966),p.15.
4. *Parkland College Student Personnel Handbook.* Prepared by Dr. Gary Armon James, Dean of Students, Parkland College, Champaign, Illinois, August, 1971,p.14.
5. e.g., *The American College Testing Proram Class Profile Norms for National Community-Junior Colleges.* The American College Testing Program, Iowa City, Fall, 1970,p.26. *Location* was a "major consideration" to 72% of the students taking ACT, and *Low Cost* a "major consideration" to 57%. Only these, *Good Faculty* and *Special Curriculum,* were important factors in the selection of the community college to more than half the students.

25

6. *Orientation '71: Students, Study Skills and You.* Learning Laboratory Committee Report, Parkland College, Champaign, Illinois, September, 1971,p.1.

7. *ADFL Bulletin* for March and September, 1970, and March, May and September, 1971. All have articles on the Doctor of Arts degree; there is also a report on the April, 1971, Conference on the Training and Orientation of Foreign Language Teachers in the Junior Colleges in the September, 1971 issue, pp.42-9.

8. Alden E. Dunham, *The Colleges of the Forgotten Americans* (New York: McGraw-Hill Book Co., 1969),p.113:

> ...at these same lower ranks,
> [salaries at] the public colleges
> and emerging universities. This
> is of great importance because it
> means that the public junior col-
> leges are highly competitive with
> the public four-year colleges when
> it comes to attracting faculty.
> An instructor at a public junior
> college with average compensation
> [in 1969] of $8,747 receives $500
> more than an instructor at a major
> university! (Junior colleges with-
> out academic ranks are not included
> in the figures.)

3.   **THE COLLEGES OF THE 80's — THE CHALLENGE
TO THE 70's**

AURORA QUIRÓS de HAGGARD
Loop Junior College
Chicago, Illinois

Let me preface my remarks by applauding Professor Louise Allen's perceptive description
of the comprehensive junior-community college,
and seconding enthusiastically the central
thrust and final challenge of her presentation.[1]

In my own statement I should like to highlight some of the points already presented and
then take a slightly different direction, as
I have tried to indicate in my title: "The
Colleges of the 80's--The Challenge to the
70's."   I shall also focus particularly on the
metropolitan junior-community college, which
by its size and the nature and complexity of
its community, is where the trends in the
community college tend to show themselves early, and where crises and problems are particularly acute.

There are at present over 1,000 community

Reprinted from the *ADFL Bulletin,* Vol. III,
No.3 (March, 1972), pp.27-30.

colleges in the nation enrolling about 2.5
million students.[2] Continued heavy growth
is predicted for the next five to ten years
for the community colleges, and indeed, they
are the only institutions of higher education
in the country in which substantial growth is
expected. Small wonder, then, that the importance of the junior-community college is
more and more widely recognized, and that
its impact on the entire educational system
of the nation is increasingly felt.

In Illinois, where the public junior college began some sixty years ago, its growth,
after a long time of lag, is now particularly
rapid, second only to New York. There are
now in Illinois 48 junior colleges with a
total enrollment of about 170,000 full and
part-time students.[3] Of this total, over
48,000, including students in adult education
courses, are enrolled in the City Colleges
of Chicago, the metropolitan junior college
which I shall use as my base example in this
paper, the college that began in 1911 with
26 students in a few rooms of the old Crane
High School on Chicago's west side.

The two year college serving large urban
areas has all of the characteristics that
have been ascribed to the institution in general, but because of the complexity of the
metropolis which is its community, it reveals
all of these features in a unique configura-
tion. Let me describe as an example the
City Colleges of Chicago. There are seven
tuition-free semi-autonomous Colleges in the
Chicago Junior college system, plus a "TV
College" offering courses on television for
college credit, plus an Urban Skills Center
teaching basic job-entry skills to unemployed
adults.

The campuses are located throughout the

city, and each College reflects and is responsive to the particular neighborhoods, the community, in which it is located. Three of the
Colleges have a predominantly black student
population, three are predominantly white.
One, the College on which I shall focus specifically, The Loop College, located in the
heart of downtown Chicago, has a racial distribution of students which "almost exactly
mirrors the racial composition of college-age
youth of the city,"[4] with the largest number
of students of Spanish origin of any midwest
college (roughly 7% of our total enrollment
of about 10,000) and the second largest number of black students of any college in the
Chicago area. The racial-ethnic-cultural diversity of the College is further reflected
in the number of Oriental American, American
Indian and foreign students. Of the latter,
there are over 350 at Loop College this semester, representing 44 different countries.
The students we teach range in age from 16 to
70, with 30% over the age of 25. They come
from the entire metropolitan area--inner city,
middle class and Lake Shore neighborhoods, as
well as from 60 suburban communities.[5]

As in most public junior colleges, most
of our students work, many full time, and
choose the City College for reasons of time
limitation as well as for economic reasons.
But to understand the particular teaching
challenge of our kind of college it is also
important to note that in a metropolis like
Chicago, where there do exist relatively inexpensive four-year institutions, easily accessible by public transportaion, a very considerable number of our college-age students
are drawn primarily for academic reasons to
the City College. For them it is the college
with the open door, with the commitment to
comprehensiveness and to maintaining a balance
of opportunities for everyone, as well as to

29

making available supportive and remedial services not usually found in more conventional
institutions--study habits seminars, one-to-
one tutoring programs,[6] career conseling,
pre-collegiate preparatory courses, and even
GED preparation for non-high school graduates.

There is no question that a highly diverse body of students presents a continuous
challenge to the faculty and the administrators of a public metropolitan junior college.
Some of our students are transfer-directed,
of course; many are interested primarily in
vocational-technical training, others in
upgrading job skills, some in taking a course
or two now and then for self-improvement,
others in taking advantage of programs designed specifically to meet community, ethnic or
other special interests. Currently, in addition to its on-campus offerings, The Loop
College conducts classes at some 46 off-cam-
pus locations: community centers, churches,
government offices, factories. And just recently Chancellor Oscar E. Shabat announced
to the press that if the Chicago Board of Education drops its 30,000-student adult education program, the City Colleges may take it
on, if funding can be found for the program.

In the many-faceted student and community
commitments of an urban community college,
foreign languages can and do play an important role. Let me mention just a few aspects
of our program as examples.

At the request of the Chicago Police Department, we have taught Spanish in the squad
room of the 13th District police station to
officers training for work in the Puerto Rican, Cuban, and Mexican-American communities
of the city. We regularly teach elementary
Spanish to civil servants in many government

30

departments and agencies which relate to the
Spanish-speaking communities of Chicago.
Special language classes are given to employ-
ees of the Chicago Public Library and of the
Mayor's Commission on Economic and Cultural
Development. We have taught a course in
"The Sounds of English" specifically for na-
tive speakers of Spanish; and, in answer to
requests from residents of a predominantly
Slavic-American neighborhood into which
Spanish-speaking families were moving, we
have taught "Let's Speak Spanish with our
Neighbors" at a community center. We added
Swahili to the languages we offer during the
time when Black Studies were an important
part of the demands of our black students.

An increasingly important development
throughout the nation is bilingual education.
Our courses in Modern Hebrew, in Japanese, in
Italian have attracted a clientele from all
parts of the city. The course "Spanish for
Hispano-americanos" filled and closed with a
waiting list early in this semester's registration period. At present, we are investigating the possibility of offering Polish for
Americans of Polish descent, and also exploring with the Business Department of the College the development of programs for bilingual secretaries.

Another important trend for community
junior college language departments, English
and foreign, is the increasing demand for
the teaching of English as a second language.
One third of the foreign language staff of
Loop College, many of whom are tri-lingual,
teach also in the English programs at the
College for native speakers of other languages. Fifty selected students from other
nations are currently enrolled in two full-
time, team-taught programs. There could easily be more if money, space, and staff were

available. In addition, eleven sections of
courses in English for speakers of other
languages are offered during the day and
evening. (Incidentally, the City Colleges
of Chicago operate throughout the year, from
eight o'clock in the morning until ten at
night.)

I have described at some length a few of
the perhaps relatively less common activities
of a department of foreign languages of a
particular urban community college because I
believe they are examples of trends which are
being felt, or will be, across the nation in
our kind of institution. These trends present opportunities we must further explore,
develop, and improve, especially if enrollment in more traditional foreign language
courses decreases, as is generally predicted.
Ours, except on 101 levels, *is* declining;
our attrition rate is high, as it is nation-
wide in languages, and it is a constant battle to keep from becoming a first-semester-
course department. This particular battle
will, in my opinion, be won only with the
most flexible, imaginative, creative kind of
teaching on the battlefield of present-day
reality--using a strategy that is responsive
to the needs, goals, and characteristics of
our students themselves.

Many of us who taught in inner-city public junior colleges in the tense days of direct student confrontations became aware early of some of the concepts beginning now to
be more widely recognized. The idea of accountability, for example, accountability
applicable not only to institutions with dol-
lar-input and product-output implications,
but also applicable to individuals, to teachers and their performance and effectiveness
in the classroom. I remember a student say-
ing to me four or five years ago, "If I'm

32

trying my best, studying hard as I can, and doing all the things you tell me I'm supposed to do, and I still don't get it, it's *your* fault too." A startling idea at first, but, of course, that young man was right, and his assertion very much in line with Kenneth Clark's famous observation that most of those whom the traditional educational system labels as unable to learn are, in reality, those who have never really been *taught*. The foreign language teachers at that inner-city college responded to the challenge with the most off-beat, rule-breaking, exciting result producing teaching any of us had ever done--the kind of teaching a large number of our students must and should have in order to learn, to succeed in the courses we teach.

Of course there is creative, innovative teaching in foreign languages going on today in this country, lots of it, but still much too rare, especially on post-high school levels, undoubtedly because relatively little attention is given to preparation for *teaching* on levels beyond the high school. It is obvious that authoritarian, lock-step, book-bound language teaching does not work--certainly not in the community junior college. Yet many of us are still caught in this approach, whatever we may say we do, however elaborately we may design our language laboratories. I remember suggesting to a group of junior college language professors not too long ago that since the bulk of our enrollment was in the 101 courses of all the languages we offered, it would be well to address ourselves to the idea of restructuring the 101 course so that it had value and educational validity in itself, and did not exist *only* as preparation for the 102 course which almost 50% of those thaking 101 did not elect to take. The suggestion was met with resistance, anxiety, and defensiveness--and

33

with much talk about maintaining "standards."

But there are many pressures today which will not allow us this kind of "luxury," among them a real financial crisis, increasing self-examination within our own ranks, and some responsible student involvement which I hope will lead us, or indeed force us to undertake some long overdue rethinking and reform. Students were the major impetus to change in education in this country in the 60's, and today are effectively asserting their right to be taught so that they *do* learn, the right to evaluate their instructors (why not?), and the right to have a responsible share in many, or all, aspects of the educational process of which they are the central part.

During the critical days of black student revolt in the inner-city junior college at which I taught in the 60's, where a number of professors -and indeed the president of the college- were ousted by student force, an important part of the screening of the applicants for teaching Swahili was a demonstration lesson that each candidate was asked to present to a group of students representing those who had indicated they would take Swahili when offered. The student groups discussed and evaluated the performance of each applicant, and voted. I found the judgment of the students excellent, and the person hired to teach Swahili was their first choice, and also the applicant, who, in my own evaluation independently arrived at, with the help of the usual academic documents and references, was indeed the superior candidate.

The history of the public community junior college and its stunningly rapid growth help to account for many of its unique char-

acteristics, its contradictions, and the
problems it faces--problems of money, of
space, of faculty and programs, of attitudes
and objectives, as well as tensions that often divide our own house. These tensions,
in turn, derive from communication and credibility gaps among and between groups and in-
dividuals--faculty, taxpayers, governing
boards, administrators, legislators, and
students. Because of an abundance, at times
an overabundance of students, we have to
some extent simply grown wild, and it is now
time to take stock.

The community junior college began, not
so long ago, as an extension of the high
school, the thirteenth and fourteenth years
as it were, It quickly identified itself
with "higher education," however, with the
lower division of four-year institutions,
and at present we are characterized by elements of both high school and university
systems. This is reflected not only in our
structure and clientele, but also in us, the
faculty, in the ways we teach and in our
self-image. As Robert Blackburn of the Center for the Study of Higher Education at the
University of Michigan has pointed out, the
community junior college tends to think of
itself as a scholarly institution and requests sabbaticals, tenure, and other benefits afforded instructors at four-year institutions; at the same time, however, it claims
that it is primarily a teaching institution
whose faculty, therefore, should not be expected to engage in research or publication.
We are members of the AAUP, but we have also
organized into labor unions. We proclaim
that teaching, good teaching, is our main
concern, but valid evaluation of performance
has so far eluded us, and therefore promotion
in the academic ranks, with titles adopted
from the university system, and even increases

in salary, are often based on the attainment
of traditional research degrees, or the accumulation of graduate credits for courses which
in most cases, interesting though they may be,
are irrelevant to our needs in meeting the
demands of the jobs we do in our particular
kind of institution.

Relatively few of the thousands of teachers now serving in the community colleges of
the nation had ever had any real contact with
the institution before becoming a part of it.
Some had taught in high shcool, others in
university and four-year colleges; a large
number came with no teaching experience at
all, directly from graduate training designed
primarily to produce scholars and professors
for situations very different from that of
the junior college. I would hazard the opinion that it is a very small percentage indeed
of the present community college faculty
nationwide, or of today's applicants for jobs
in the community-junior college, that has ever
had any training specifically for the junior
college--or for teaching at all. And very
few opportunities exist even now for the preparation of faculty for this unique and increasingly important institution of our
society.

Of the qualities which Professor Allen has
cited as indispensable for community college
teaching, I would underline flexibility and
imagination, qualities which enable a teacher
to cope with many kinds of teaching and people,
to be adventuresome in exploring what to do
and when and how, to look at language in non-
authoritarian terms. With this in mind, I
would stress training in methodology, with direct experience in the junior college situation, in comparative and applied linguistics,
in courses like Professor Raven McDavid's
"Problems of Urban Speech" at the University

of Chicago, and contemporary courses in sociology, language learning, and urban problems. Keep in mind, by the way, that "urban problems" are spreading at a frightening speed to what used to be considered non-urban areas.

Undoubtedly the most dramatic educational challenge to the 70's is the *faculty* for the colleges of the 80's. Many of us now in the system, by luck, accident, or natural agility and love of teaching, have somehow survived and even thrived on the experience of sailing choppy, unfamiliar waters; others of us have only survived, in some measure because of tenure, an institution recently more and more under scrutiny.

Without question, the political, social and educational climate in this country today, together with increased student awareness and uneasiness within the academic profession itself, plus, of course, serious economic pressures, mark the 70's as the crucial time for change. In our own field, there are signs that both the community colleges and the four-year and graduate institutions are beginning to reexamine seriously both undergraduate and graduate education in foreign languages, and to plan for academically sound, respectable and respected relevant, non-traditional degrees and programs for junior college teachers. The concerns and resolutions of the ADFL 1971 Summer Seminar are promising cases in point. And there are many other signs in the wind throughout the nation--including the work of a committee of the Illinois Association of Community and Junior Colleges presently studying the problem of graduate programs specifically designed for community-junior college teachers in training, and also for teachers already in service, in their own academic fields.

If we can, with intelligence and flexibility, meet the challenge of the 70's, then the Colleges of the 80's. the public community-junior college, will truly be where the action is--not only because masses of students and educators will be involved in lots of "activity," but because -to borrow a phrase from the students- we've finally gotten it all together into well-directed, productive action.

NOTES

1. See L. Allen, "The Colleges of the 80's--or Where the Action Is."
2. "Community College Trends," *Illinois Association of Community and Junior Colleges Faculty Division Newsletter*, III,Div.3, No.1,Oct.1971.
3. Kurt A. Klein, "The Teaching of Foreign Languages in the Illinois Public Junior Colleges," *The University of Illinois Foreign Language Newsletter*, XXIV,7-8, April-May,1971
4. David H. Heller, *"Getting It All Together,"* address presented at his inauguration as president of The Loop College, 18,Oct.1970.
5. *The Loop College Institutional Self-Study and Profile.* Prepared by the Office of Planning, Research and Evaluation, Dr. Maurice Kessman, director. April,1971.
6. The Department of Foreign Languages at The Loop College has organized two supportive tutoring programs: one, a volunteer "language-exchange" program involves Americans studying foreign languages and native speakers of foreign languages who are studying English as a second language at the College; the second, a scheduled program, uses paid student tutors working under supervision to help students of foreign languages who

need or want additional practice or conversation on a personal one-to-one basis.

SECTION II:

PROCEEDINGS OF

THE ILLINOIS CONFERENCE ON FOREIGN LANGUAGES

IN JUNIOR AND COMMUNITY COLLEGES

4. CONSERVATION AND INNOVATION

WILGA M. RIVERS
University of Illinois

In *Precaution*, Robert Frost has said:

> I never dared be radical when young
> For fear it would make me conservative
> when old.[1]

At first reading I found this rather startling but on reflection, it linked in my mind
with a recent statement of Gunter Grass:
"I think there are many realities, and all
these realities can exist at the same time."[2]
Radicals and conservatives converge in be-
lieving that they have *the* answer, that there
is one right approach to a question, whereas
effective foreign language teaching in diverse
institutions at the present time must accept
the reality of many *answers*, to be selected
according to the diversity of need and cir-

circumstance. In this article, then, I am not speaking of conservatism or radicalism, but of the interplay in any evolving situation between conservation and innovation.

We at the University of Illinois at Urbana have just won what we see as a significant victory[3]: to conserve something we believe to be a valuable part of our students' educational experience.[4] Conservation is not merely clinging blindly to the old and the established because it is the known and the secure. Conservation means recognizing that something has value and working actively for its survival. For anything to survive it must be able to respond to new circumstances and new demands. Innovation, then, is essential to conservation if that which we believe to be of value is not to become a mere museum piece, retained for reasons of prestige although no longer serving a useful purpose in its changed setting.

What, then, are we conserving? Why did we at the University of Illinois at Urbana work so hard to preserve foreign language study as an essential element in liberal education? As educators, we wished to conserve for all liberally-educated students the opportunity to get outside of their own language, to get outside of the thought-molds of their native culture, to get outside of their own value systems, if only momentarily, in order to see their own ways of thinking and expressing themselves, their own conceptions of the normal and the obvious, their own responses to situations and ideas and people from a different perspective.

This is something which we feel to be worth conserving in the education of the individual, because it develops a flexibility

of thinking which is becoming more and more
essential for all as we are challenged daily
by the continally evolving ideas, values,
and demands of a fast-changing society.[5]
Broadening our perspective from individual to
societal needs, and bringing its implications
nearer home, we may through this effect on
individuals contribute to the breaking down
of that "provincialism and parochialism which
threaten a nation which feels psychologically
isolated from its neighbors,"[6] and which, as
a result, may tend to turn in on itself instead of facing boldly the challenges of new
concepts and new relationships.

Conservation, then, refers to the values
of foreign language study, innovation to
their realization in a new setting in a new
decade, and you in the junior and community
colleges are right in the midst of this new
opportunity.

If students of today with their yearning
to roam, physically and spiritually, beyond
national boundaries and their questioning of
traditional values do not enjoy learning a
foreign language, then (to parallel Shakespeare):

> The fault, dear [friends], is not in our
>   [subject],
> But in ourselves that we are underlings.[7]

An unadulterated diet of frankly preliminary
learnings for persons who will never reach
the consummatory stage is indigestible and
unpalatable--yet, this is what many of our
students are served and served exclusively.
In two-year colleges, this means what is fund-
amentally a transfer program for non-trans-
fers, or at least non-majors.[8] We talk glib-
ly about our objectives and our goals, but in
our step-by-step program for foreign language

45

mastery these goals are only dimly perceived as attainable, even after several arduous semesters of tedious grind. Student motivation, whose apparent lack we often deplore, is stimulated and channeled, not by the setting out of reasonable and relevant objectives which salve the instructor's conscience, but by student perception of the attainment and attainability of those objectives.[9]

It is here that the junior and community colleges can, and should, lead the way. A two-year college is not an elitist institution drawing on the top ten percent of the high school graduating class. It is not an established institution sunk deep in ivy and centuries of habit. It is a new concept with a new clientele and should be pulsating with new life. As foreign language teachers we may consider that this new clientele needs this age-old experience as much as, and perhaps more than, the traditional college population. We will wish to conserve the essence of the language learning experience in this new institution. This does not mean that we have to, or can necessarily, conserve the forms, the institutionalized modes, of initiating students into this experience. Junior and community college instructors must innovate: they must experiment in renewing the forms while retaining the essence. Content, organization of learning experiences, modality of learning, pace, and gauging of progress should all be reexamined in order to make accessible to all kinds of students this unique educational experience of encounter with another way of thought and expression.

Such innovation requires understanding, imagination, and courage.

UNDERSTANDING (perceptiveness): to see what the student needs, not in a utilitarian sense, but in a human sense.

IMAGINATION: thinking beyond the confines
of past and present experience; assessing,
in relation to the needs of the students,
possibilities which have never been tried.

COURAGE: to know the students as they
are, to recognize what must be provided
for them and to accept them as full partners in their own educational experience;
courage to do what has not been done before and is not being done elsewhere;
courage to accept the mistakes you have
made and learn from them; courage to with-
stand the criticsim of others who remain
safely on well-trodden paths.

The junior and community colleges are, for
the most part, young. Let them also be ad-
venturous. Imagination and courage come more
easily to the young.

At this conference let us drop our masks
with each other and share freely, allowing
imagination and insight to flow from one to
another, so that we may develop new patterns
and new attitudes appropriate to our new situation. What matter if we are called *dreamers*!
All the great innovators have been dreamers.
We need the courage to set down our convic-
tions, to work them through realistically, and
to return to our colleges ready to insist on
our right to experiment rationally, with the
equanimity to face criticism, indifference,
and discouragement as we try to implement our
ideas. Of course, we will make mistakes; of
course, some of our ideas will not work, but
all progress comes through experimentation.
Each failure provides as much information as
a success when we function as a sharing, mutually comprehensive community.

47

PRACTICAL SUGGESTIONS

Here without wishing to direct your thinking into preselected channels, I would like
to present several concepts of curriculum
planning which are worth careful consideration: Continuing and Terminal Courses; The
Hors d'Oeuvre Approach; Diversification of
Content; Variation in Pacing.

With a diverse student population we must
study carefully the questions:
Who is going where?
What does he want and need?

Our traditional foreign language courses
at college level have been *continuing
courses*[10] in the sense that they have been
designed with the mastery required of the
future major in mind. Setting the foundation
with care, building on it methodically and
soberly, they have moved steadily toward the
objective of a complete and fully equipped
edifice. At any stage on the way the edifice
is incomplete, unfunctional, only minimally
usable in a makeshift fashion. If construction ceases at an early stage, the embryonic
edifice deteriorates and finally crumbles to
dust. So it is with a continuing course--
those who go on to the stage of mastery are
well equipped, solidly grounded, able to
function in the language; those who drop out
after the foundations are laid soon forget,
finding no use for the small accumulation of
knowledge and skill which it took a great
deal of time and energy to acquire.

There is, and always will be, a place for
the continuing course--for those who want and
need it. We have many ideas for the design
and operation of such courses. But for the
others, for those who stay with us a short
while, who come to see what we have to offer

48

as our contribution to a liberal education?
Can we not do better for them?

Here the concept of *the terminal course*
can help us. A terminal course sets a goal
related to the interests and needs of the
students in that course and achieves that
goal, no matter how long or short the course
may be. The goals, then, vary. Some take
longer to achieve than others, but this is
known to and accepted by the students who
undertake the course. Is the student to remain with us only one semester? Then, instead of deploring this fact and force-feed-
ing him the usual introductory diet, we design a course which will give him a complete
experience during that semester. Here, the
hors d'oeuvre approach can be helpful. Is he
more likely to remain for four semesters?
Then we design a course in which he will have
acquired something he can perceive as an a-
chievement in those four semesters. Perhaps
he can understand films or broadcasts or take
part in general conversation at an uncompli-
cated level? Maybe he can read magazines and
newspapers or articles in a specialized field
but can do no more than find his way about
orally. At least he will not go away with
only preliminary learnings for more advanced
courses he will never take.

Once the concept of a distinction between
continuing and terminal courses is accepted,
all our planning is affected. We can then
consider the advantages of a terminal-type
first semester course which will allow some to
retire gracefully from the field, having tas-
ted to see whether foreign language study interests them, but which will motivate others
to continue because new perspectives have
opened up to them which they are anxious to
explore.

I shall call this the *Hors d'Oeuvre Course*, knowing full well that this very title will cause some to dismiss it as a frivolity which cannot be taken seriously. Such an attitude springs from a rather widespread, often subconscious, feeling that really educative activities cannot possibly be, or at least ought not to be, enjoyable. This being an attitude we should combat, let us keep the term for the present. Dictionaries sometimes translate or explain the word *hors d'oeuvre* as "little appetizers," their function being to arouse our appetite for more substantial food. One of our problems in the foreign language field is the early dropout rate, which is uncomfortably high after one or two semesters in institutions where foreign language study is purely elective. Under the present system, what do these dropouts gain, in an educational sense, after one semester?

With the *hors d'oeuvre* approach, the first semester would be designed to give each student an insight into the nature of the subject some practical experience of the language and the culture of the speakers of that language, and a feeling for the fundamental differences between languages. It would be an interesting course in itself, exciting some to continue, illuminating all on the nature of the discipline, and making a valuable, if small, contribution to the educational experience of each student. As an approach it is worth considering seriously.

Why should our foreign language menu be stodgy and unattractive? Is there any serious reason why students should not thoroughly enjoy their introduction to a language, so that they anticipate their next course with genuine pleasure? We all know that motivation is necessary to carry students through the in-

evitably solid, and sometimes tedious, learning necessary for acquiring any lasting control of a language. If the *hors d'oeuvre* approach arouses in some a real desire to learn
the language more fully, it will have made an
important contribution to the program. And
then, if those who go no further retain in
later life favorable attitudes toward the
whole language learning enterprise, this in
itself will return dividends in a gradually
improving community attitude toward the foreign language program at the college.

Beyond the introductory course, our objective should be a *diversified offering*. We
are continually being told this is the age of
pluralism. What appeared from a psychological
distance to be a monolithic society has proved
on closer examination to be a great diversity
of cultures, sub-cultures, groups, subgroups,
and individuals--each with his own goals, aspirations, and interests. The foreign language programs of the present and the future
must reflect this diversity.

In the foreign language field we are very
fortunate: language is a vehicle of expression, not an end in itself. A multiplicity of
possibilities therefore opens before us. Language which is being used purposefully will be
learned. We have, then, a multiplicity of
possible content and a multiplicity of possible activities from which to choose. Suitable
approaches and *pace of learning* can be as varied as the personalities and temperaments of
our students.[11] Language can be learned
through conversation, through reading,
through singing, through listening, from
radio, film, or drama, through translation,
through writing, by library research, by independent study, in group activities, social
activities, or community action. A diversity
of possible courses awaits the attention of

those who with imagination, energy, and confidence are willing to experiment with new structures and a new content. Where better to begin than in the junior and community colleges where the spirit of innovation is evident in the very fact of their existence?

NOTES

1. Robert Frost, "Precaution," in *Complete Poems of Robert Frost* (New York: Henry Holt & Co., 1948),p.407.
2. J. Robert Moskin, Interview with Günter Grass, "Günter Grass and the Murderer at the Desk," *Intellectual Digest*, April, 1972,p.20.
3. On March 22, 1972 the day the Illinois Conference began, the faculty of the College of Liberal Arts and Sciences at the University of Illinois at Urbana-Champaign voted by a two-thirds majority to retain the graduation and entrance requirements in foreign language of the College (four semesters of college or four years of high school study). See Richard T. Scanlan, "The Vote for the Foreign Language Requirement: Strategy Notes," in the Action Report section.
4. In this case conservation witn innovation. See Action Reports by J. McGlathery, R. Figge, and W. Rivers.
5. The problems of adapting to new attitudes among youth and rapid change in society are discussed at length in "Foreign Languages in a Time of Change" in Wilga M. Rivers, *Speaking in Many Tongues: Essays in Foreign-Language Teaching* (Rowley, Mass.: Newbury House, 1972).
6. Quoted from "Basic Information on the FL Requirement" issued by the Scanlan Committee, University of Illinois at Urbana, 1972.
7. W. Shakespeare, *Julius Caesar*, I,ii, with

adaptations.

8. Sister Marie Celeste's survey shows that of the 5,619 students in two-year college foreign language programs in Illinois in 1971-2, only 43 could be considered future foreign language majors. See article in this book.

9. The complex question of student motivation is discussed in depth in Wilga M. Rivers, "Motivating through Classroom Techniques," in *Speaking in Many Tongues* (1972), and in Chapter 9 of the *Psychologist and the Foreign-Language Teacher* (Chicago, 1964) by the same author.

10. Continuing and terminal courses are discussed (with more elaboration of content) As Stage One and Stage Two programs in Wilga M. Rivers, "Foreign Languages in a Time of Change" in *Speaking in Many Tongues* (1972).

11. A program diversified in content and pace is described in my Action Report, "Diversification of the First Four Semesters," article in this book. Most colleges would not have the possibility or the need for such an extensive program, but college instructors may gain ideas from it for adaptation to their own situation.

5. FOREIGN LANGUAGE CURRICULUM IN THE TWO-YEAR COLLEGE: WHITHER?

LOUISE H. ALLEN
Parkland Junior College
Champaign, Illinois

Recently a friend of mine dropped into my office to talk about his personal future. His personal future may happen to be bound up with the future of foreign languages in community colleges. He is a successful secondary-school teacher who is thinking of making the move to the college level, if there *is* a future there. As we talked both of us realized that we were raising more questions than we were answering.

Curriculum in foreign languages in two-year colleges -as in high school and four-year colleges- is clearly in a period of change. The traditional elementary-year, intermediate-year, advanced-year pattern is going if not already gone. My friend and I found ourselves speculating about what the new pattern might be, and hoping that this Conference might provide us with some of the answers.

Several preliminary meetings were held this past fall and winter to prepare for this Conference. The program of the Foreign Language Articulation Conference at the University of Illinois in October included a special session for members of community college faculties; regional meetings were held in January around the State of Illinois to provide specific input to this Conference. The reports of these meetings indicate that the problems of foreign language instruction in two-year colleges are exceedingly varied, but they do show a certain number of common features.

1) The "image" of foreign language study seems to be that it is difficult, irrelevant, and a pointless requirement, unrelated to the student's real desires and goals for his career and/or life style.

2) Emphasis on grammar and pattern practice in the first year is under question, if not attack, everywhere.

3) Faculty and students alike are uncertain about the best content for intermediate and advanced courses: review grammar? conversation? composition? culture and area studies? commercial? literature? or something totally new?

4) There is general uneasiness about placement of students who have had several years of FLES, junior high school and high school language study; and there is parallel concern about placement of students who have studied a language in the past, have been out of contact with it for several years, and who now seek to resume it.

5) There is concern about the growing non-English-speaking and bilingual communi-

ties in our cities: whether we are either
strengthening their knowledge of their first
language or helping to prepare service people
to assist their transition into American culture.

Overhanging this morass are two potential
avalanches threatening disaster: namely,
sliding enrollments and sliding budgets.
Universities are reducing or abandoning foreign language requirements, being pressured
to do so. Our own funding for non-credit
courses has been all but cut off by state
legislative action. Funding for credit
courses may be next to go. Small numbers of
our students enter the foreign language program, and even smaller numbers finish it;
many withdraw before the end of the first
course. Part-time staffing has become almost
routine.

The central questions about curriculum
of this Conference then, I think, become:
How can we in the community colleges get
students to be interested in foreign language
offerings in the first place, and how can we
keep them long enough for them to develop
some useful knowledge or skill to carry away?

Simply posing those questions suggests a
number of other questions.

1) Is it realistic to try to teach a
grammar-oriented course to students whose
acquaintance with English is largely on the
level of usage, and with whom we must begin
by teaching the jargon of grammar: What is
a noun? What is agreement? person? number?
tense? And, worst of all, the subjunctive?

2) How good for our students is pattern
practice? One of the regional meetings leading to this Conference reported "the most re-

sounding and repeated refrain was that learning by rote is an acceptable approach for the
student who intends to pursue languages as
an area of concentration. For the majority,
however, more emphasis on culture and life
styles might have the greatest appeal and
most relevance."[1]

3) Should our second-year courses continue to be, as many of them now are described
in our catalogs, "a review of grammar and the
beginning of free conversation"?[2] Or should
free conversation be introduced from the
first day, as it is in some of our courses
for prospective travelers? (Parenthetically,
I find myself recalling my American landlady
in Mexico, who had lived there and conducted
a successful business for some twenty years,
but whose unique Spanish verb form was the
infinitive!)

4) Is the traditional second-year reader,
a collection of short stories with perhaps
a few poems and/or personal essays, or a
novel, the most appropriate material to give
our intermediate students? Or should we look
more to newspapers, magazines, personal correspondence, meeting speakers of the language
face to face? Or examine air pollution in
Paris, road-building in Peru, folk-dance in
Bern?

5) What are we doing for our advanced
students--those who come to us with several
years' experience of the language, either in
school or perhaps by foreign residence? Are
the obstacles presently set before us by administrative procedures, both within and without the college, effectively depriving these
students of further language training which
they desire and deserve?

6) What service are we giving, or should

we give, to our students with specialized
needs: The policeman who may work in a Spanish neighborhood? The nurse who may serve
Spanish- or Polish-speaking patients? The
traveler who wants to learn to read foreign
menus and handle foreign money? The chef
who needs to learn to read Greek, or Italian,
or Chinese, or French recipes? The Japanese
or German neighborhood group who want to perfect their control of the written language
and seek instruction in its literature?

7) How can we relate most effectively
with senior institutions, whose foreign language programs are also in trouble? Must we
(and they) continue to worry about "maintaining standards," which often translates to
"finishing the textbook in a given period of
time"? (Again parenthetically, I remember
the university professor who inquired at one
of the regional meetings, *"Why* are those
books so long, anyway!")[3] Must we (and they)
continue to program lock-step curricula,
rather than tailoring courses to student
needs and interests, in order to insure transfer credit for our graduates? Or if we feel
we need to track some of our students into
terminal courses, shouldn't those students
have the assurance that they will not be
forced into further required foreign language
at the senior institution?[4] Shouldn't we and
our university colleagues talk together about
placement arrangements, transition courses,
and flexible credit and transfer systems?
And shouldn't students at both community and
senior colleges be brought into these discussions?

8) What does that word that we hear more
and more these days--*accountability*--mean for
us? Cost-effectiveness? (A potential threat
to our small classes and high degree of individual attention.) Transfer success and

performance on standardized tests? (A possible argument against experimentation.) Student interest or disaffection? (A real concern, in the light of our low enrollments and high attrition rates.) The third volume of the *Britannica Review of Foreign Language Education* recommends "cautions...with this concept [accountability]"[5] but administrators, boards and legislatures seem delighted with it. Is there food for thought for us here?

9) Do we need new materials as well as new approaches? And if so, whence should we seek them? Should we generate them ourselves? Or offer guidelines and advice to publishers and established authors? Or both? And what *kinds* of materials should we look to? Textbooks? Workbooks? Slide-and-cassette series? Programmed worksheets? Or none of the above?

These are the kinds of questions my friend and I found ourselves wrestling with.

Let me suggest a possible approach to solving some of these problems: namely, that we take a leaf from the book of our colleagues in career programs, and employ a "hands-on" approach to foreign language classes. Language learning is basically skill-acquisition, and therefore has some common features with learning to weld, run computers, or keep accounts. Our vocational-technical colleagues who teach those skills take the view that "all students should have real experience in their technology *at the beginning of the program*" (italics mine).[6] Can we not also give our students real experience with the language at the beginning of the program, rather than a series of abstract paradigms and contrived dialogues? Most of us would like to, I think, but wonder how to get started.

One way of doing this is the *student pro-ject technique*. One widely-read text on learning theory says flatly, "Where possible, through the medium of a democratic classroom climate, a teacher's task is to help induce personal involvement."[7]

We know that our students like direct in-volvement in their own learning, and that such involvement pays off in improved atti-tudes toward subject matter. We also know that attitude is particularly important in language learning.[8] The project approach permits students to design and carry out sub-stantial parts of their own learning experi-ences, individually and/or in groups. Those of us who have experimented with it have been delighted with the energy and enthusiasm that students put into projects and with the solid learning that results from them. And we have found that students can do many things with a foreign language surprisingly early in their study of it.

In the first few weeks of the elementary course, some students can please the palates of their classmates with a tasty dish pre-pared from a recipe in a foreign newspaper or magazine, and learn the names of many foods and the metric system *en route*. Others can describe a simple picture or transparency, or plot and explain on maps a trip they have made or would like to make. Others may exa-mine traffic signs or gestures and explain and demonstrate them. Still others may want to learn a song or folk dance and teach it to the class.

A few weeks later, with a little help, students can write and present a dialogue of their own, perhaps in the form of a skit or

puppet show. Others may choose to design an
easy crossword puzzle or teach a card game
or Scrabble in the language. Some may want
to improve their own vocabularies by analyzing a lesson or story for cognates, word-
roots, prefixes and suffixes; distributing
their materials will help their classmates,
too. Others may enjoy re-recording the laboratory tapes with splices of music they have
chosen, or synchronizing tape material with
slides they have selected, or augmenting
tapes with conversations with native speakers
of their acquaintance. (Obviously, any device that gets students to *listen* to those
tapes is a point for us!)

Each class invents new kinds of projects,
which neither the instructor nor other classes have thought of before, so the stock of
ideas constantly grows.

The project-oriented class has, by the
end of the first quarter or semester considerable knowledge of the culture of the country or countries where the language is
spoken and control over some aspects of the
language itself. Individual students have a
sense of having contributed to the course,
and have something to carry away with them
even if they leave the study of the language
at this point. Most have also developed
some curiosity about the finer points of the
language and therefore a desire to continue
studying it.

For us as instructors to encourage our
students to design their own projects takes a
bit of courage, of course. The technique
runs directly contrary to the orderly, step-
by-step presentation of pronunciation, vocabulary and syntax that most of us are accustomed to. Testing and grading become real
challenges to our ingenuity. The textbook

and workbook we often depend so much on become secondary appendages if not quite unnecessary frills.

But consider the rewards: Student attendance and responsiveness tend to improve.
Students begin to seek out native speakers
and advanced students to help them with
their projects. Library and media materials
which have been carefully assembled but seldom used begin to be utilized. Projects naturally reflect individual areas of interest
and knowledgeability, so the pace and content
of the course become varied, and complaints
of irrelevancy and dull repetitiveness drop
off or cease. Some students are spared the
stigma of being "behind" others, and both
students and teacher are sparred the psychological pressure of "getting through" an ar-
bitrary number of units and structures.

Once the project-orientation of the language course has been established, it can be
built on for the remainder of the student's
stay at the college. This suggests *student
specialization* in an area or aspect of the
language. The future nurse may concentrate
on medical vocabulary and idiom; the policeman on street-slang and legal terms; the
language-major-to-be on composition and the
literature; the traveler on sights to see,
hotels to stay in and people to meet when he
gets there; the businessman or woman on commercial terms and business letter styles.
But each should *share* his knowledge *with the
class as a whole*, regularly and on a continuing basis--and *in the language*. In other
words, the students should teach the class on
a rotating basis; the instructor thus becomes
a valued resource person rather than a combination of cynosure, cheerleader and cox-
swain.

62

With this approach students of varying
levels of ability, divergent interests, and
different kinds of experience of the language
can be brought together in the same classroom and *learn from each other* as well as
from the teacher, the textbook and the tapes.
They will discover, at different rates to be
sure, that all of them need the basic patterns of grammar and a general vocabulary in
the language. They will find that they can
drop out of the language class for a time,
if illness, financial necessity, or the pressure of other courses requires it, and re-
join it at some later date without waiting a
semester or a year; and that they can move
ahead at their own pace.

We teachers should find here a blending
of our credit and non-credit courses and
help with our problems of pacing and individualization. Hopefully, we would also find
more students joining our elementary classes
and more staying on for intermediate and advanced work. Even if more students overall
did not appear, the need for justifying to
deans and cost experts tiny sections in each
of four or five courses each term should
evaporate.

Of course there arises inevitably the
question of transferability for at least
some of our students. Suppose the student
who has become an "expert" in street-language
encounters a very traditional literature-and-
correct-language department at the university;
what happens to him? Suppose the student who
has concentrated on commercial language and
style finds that he is expected to comment
intelligently on poetry or classic drama;
what is his fate? These are questions which
we need to discuss in depth with our colleagues at the senior institutions, at this
Conference and beyond it.

But they are not questions which should
paralyze us into inaction. Senior institutions, too, are experimenting these days, and
welcome fresh ideas. The Spanish and Social
Work Departments of the University of Illinois, for example, have designed a master's
degree program for bilingual social workers;[9]
our street-slang specialist would be a strong
candidate for such a program. Eastern Illinois University has "transition" courses[10]
for students of varied backgrounds in all
foreign languages; these should be ideal ve-
hicules for our students to broaden their
personal approach to the language if that
seems desirable. Northern Illinois University
describes its advanced conversation courses
as giving "special emphasis on the student's
ability to function in the [language] speaking society"[11]; our hotel-and personal-ac-
quaintance "expert" should fit in well there.
And of course many of our students will terminate their formal study of foreign language at the community college in any case,
whether they transfer or not, and whether or
not we regard them as terminal students
while they are with us. So the much-touted
"transfer problem" is very likely more apparent than real. Certainly it should not
prevent us from trying a fresh approach.

The project-oriented course is one possible kind of new foreign language curriculum for the community college, with which I
have experimented successfully myself. Certainly other participants in this Conference
have tried other approaches and had success
with them. Let us hear about them in our
discussion sections at this Conference, and
continue exploration of these and others in
the future.

We in the community colleges pride ourselves on our student-centeredness and on our

imaginative, non-traditional attitudes toward teaching and learning. Clearly, we ourselves and the foreign language profession at large would welcome some new ideas at this juncture. So let us in this Conference attempt to provide some answers, however tentative, to the question heading this paper: Foreign Language Curriculum...Whither?, and to all the other questions depending from that one. My friend making the career decision and many other concerned foreign language teachers will thank us!

NOTES

1. Report of the regional meeting held January 7, 1972, at DuPage College, Palatine, Illinois.
2. *Parkland College Catalog*, 1972-73, Champaign, Illinois,p.158. (Description of Intermediate Spanish I, used in the same catalog since 1967-68. Blushingly admitting responsibility for this one, I suggest readers look at their own catalog descriptions.)
3. Report of the regional meeting held January 14, 1972, at Parkland College, Champaign, Illinois.
4. Reports of the regional meetings held January 11, 1972, at Waubonsee Community College, Sugar Grove, Illinois.
5. Dale L. Lange, "Introduction and Overview. Pluralism in Foreign Language Education," in *Britannica Review of Foreign Language Education*, III (Chicago: Encyclopedia Britannica, Inc., 1971), p.7; and the article referred to: P.Paul Parent and Frederick P. Veidt, "Program Evaluation: Accountability," in the same volume, pp.311-31.
6. *Status and Self Studies Report*, Parkland College, Champaign, Illinois,1971,p.10.

7. Morris L. Bigge, *Learning Theories for Teachers*, 2nd ed. (New York: Harper & Row, 1971),p.280.
8. Wallace E. Lambert and Robert C. Gardner, *Attitudes and Motivation in Second Language Learning* (Rowley, Mass.: Newbury House, 1972).
9. Information is available from Prof. J.H.D. Allen Jr., Coordinator of Graduate Programs, Department of Spanish, Italian and Portuguese, University of Illinois, Urbana, Illinois.
10. Information is available from Prof. Martin Miess, Head, Department of Foreign Languages, Eastern Illinois University, Charleston, Illinois.
11. Northern Illinois University. *Undergraduate Catalog*, DeKalb, Illinois, 1971-72,pp.52-4.

5. FOREIGN LANGUAGE CURRICULUM
    IN THE TWO-YEAR COLLEGE: A RESPONSE

PETER RUSSO
DuPage Junior College
Glen Ellyn, Illinois

Essentially, Mrs. Allen's paper deals with the future of foreign languages in the community college in view of the problems that confront us. She has outlined many of these problems and has offered some good suggestions as to how they might be solved. Incidentally, these are not problems that solely face the community college instructor. They are equally pertinent to the profession in the senior institution in that both our positions are a little less tenable than they were a few years back.

Let's take a look at some of the things that presently ail us.

First, perhaps, is that of our own image. For various reasons throughout the years it has now become a rather grim and dismal one. Students are labeling the skills that we wish

to peddle as too difficult, irrelevant and
sometimes even pointless. Surprisingly, "Let
them learn English" is not an uncommon refrain in the community college. Even more
startling than this, of course, is when we
hear some of our administrators hint at the
very same thing. How do we sell innovative
language programs to administrators who may
harbor this kind of sentiment and who are
basically vocational-career program oriented,
and to students, many of whom come from blue
collar families where aesthetic values and
academia are not bywords? It's a monumental
task and one with which we grapple daily.

Another serious problem with which we are
faced is that of content. Because of the
pressure that we feel from our image and the
urgent need that we feel to change that image,
we wrestle with content. How do we make the
course enticing and relevant? How do we whet
students' appetite and make them want to go
on?

Next of course comes the matter of place-
ment--especially of those students who have
had several years of exposure to foreign languages, whether with FLES, or in junior high
or high school, or perhaps even with all
three. And another matter of great concern
is whether or not we are meeting the needs
of the community which we were founded to
serve. Finally, as though we didn't have
enough to ponder and be concerned with, Mrs.
Allen points out that there are two potential
avalanches threatening disaster which over-
hang the present state of affairs, and those,
of course, are sliding enrollments and sliding budgets.

These are only a few of the many questions
that we ask ourselves daily, and those which
cause us great consternation and sometimes

downright frustration. I would hope that we
could discuss some of these issues and take
some kind of united stance. Let's try to
spell some things out and have some better
ideas of the direction that we wish to take.
These are crucial problems which we definitely should explore here at this Conference.
The reduction, and in many cases the elimin-
ation, of language requirements in many senior institutions has made as unquestionable
mark on enrollments; in some cases it may be
threatening our very existence. Some of our
regular, or traditional offerings are teeter-
ing and falling by the wayside. How do we
combat this threat? Do we entreat the senior institutions to reinstate language requirements? Do we exert pressure to get
other requirements eliminated, so that foreign language will be in a fairer competitive
position? Or do we revamp, redirect, redesign our courses to make them more attractive
to the potential language student? Perhaps
a combination of all of these is in order.

Another great concern of the community
college teacher for a long time has been the
matter of transfer. Are we giving the students the kind of training they need to be
successful in the senior institution? Mrs.
Allen feels, as I'm sure many of us do, that
perhaps we have been overly concerned with
the transfer question, often at the expense
of our students' needs and interests. She
further points out, and I am inclined to
agree, that this concern is sometimes more
imagined than real, particularly in view of
the fact that senior institutions which have
similar problems to our own have created
"transition courses" designed to pick up the
students wherever they are in terms of ability or training. They are no longer prescrib-
ing the dosage of language that students
should have before they will accept them.

69

They, too, have enrollment problems and are just as happy to get students as we are.

What are some of the possible solutions to these problems? Mrs. Allen suggests the *student project technique*, which induces personal involvement. No doubt -as she points out- the implementation of this kind of program requires courage and ingenuity on the part of the instructor, but she maintains that the rewards are great. She states that student attendance and responsiveness tend to improve--and believe me, anything that can do that in a community college has to be dynamic! She points out another advantage in student projects is that materials which normally gather dust begin to be utilized and, even more importantly than that, the student is spared the stigma of being behind others; and it may facilitate transfer, particularly if the receiving institution is operating under a similar plan.

Once the project orientation has been established, the student can then specialize in a particular area or aspect of the language whcih he is best suited for or more interested in. The policeman, the nurse, the traveler, the businessman, and others can pursue the vocabulary which can best serve him. Each, however, must share his discoveries and knowledge with the others in the class on a continuing basis. She maintains further that this approach allows us to put students on varying levels of ability into the same classroom, thereby possibly eliminating several very small section, which have traditionally been difficult to justify to deans and cost experts. Mrs. Allen is quick to identify the transferability problem with such a plan, but she is optimistic noting that the senior institutions are exper-

imenting with fresh ideas and that perhaps
they would be more receptive that we might
expect. Furthermore, in spite of all obstacles, the community college instructor is
committed to experimentation and exploration
simply because we are student-centered and
are not traditional in our attitudes toward
teaching and learning.

To all this I would agree, but I do have
some reservations about such a plan on a
large scale. First of all, there are many
community college students uncommitted to
any kind of specialization. They have no
burning desire to explore any particular aspect of language. They are there, they want
to learn, but they don't really know what it
is that they want to learn. For this type
of student to decide on a meaningful project
for himself would take more time than is
available, and would tax the instructor's ingenuity beyond the wildest imagination. I
personally would want to provide the project
approach to students after they have had a
certain amount of exposure and have aquired
some degree of sophistication with the language. They are then better equipped to decide which areas of the language they need
more work in, would like more work in, or in
which they have the greatest interest.

Another great obstacle, as I see it, is
the manner in which we traditionally label
our language courses--Beginning Spanish 101,
Intermediate Spanish 201, etc. It is rather
expected by administrators, local school
boards, and senior institutions that language courses bear these classifications and
that a particular kind of activity take place
within them. Can you imagine the confusion
and hostility that would erupt at Northern
Illinois University if one student transferred in with credit in *Student Project in Span-*

71

ish 123? Until we are given *carte blanche*
in the matter of labeling courses and, more
importantly, in the matter of giving our students what we think professionally appropriate, we will be continually hamstrung by the
lock-step approach.

I personally like the individualized approach that Mrs. Allen recommends and I honestly think it's the way we have to go. We
need first, however, to be relieved of certain pressures that presently exist. We have
to be allowed to label our courses in ways
that would have appeal and which would suggest to our students that they aren't going
to get the dosage of language in the community college in the same way that they got it
in high school. If we are going to individualize and provide for different interests
and needs, our catalogs should clearly indicate this in their course descriptions.
Furthermore, these have to be accepted totally by the senior institution.

Students already have preconceived notions
about language 101 or 201, whereas they might
not have with Spanish Project 101, or even
Spanish Wilderness Encounter 101. Does this
sound far out??? Maybe not--we do have at
the College of DuPage a course called Wilderness Encounter, and it is attracting students
simply because they find the name intriguing
and exotic. And do you know what? Many students do pick courses because "I like the way
it sounds"--or"it sounds like it may be interesting."

In conclusion, the problems of developing
a viable foreign language curriculum in the
two-year college are many faceted and difficult to solve. We have a unique student population with objectives different from those
in the senior institutions. To pattern our

classes after those from which we, the teachers, have come, or in the tradition of the senior institution, is sheer folly. We must re-evaluate, redesign, and experiment. We must know our community and find out what the needs are and then tailor our courses to fit those needs. In many cases this will mean a total break with traditional course content and methodology. It means that we must come up with fresh, new material which allows the kind of flexibility and individualization which are urgently needed. We should be thinking about writing our own programs and texts and veer from the traditional dependency on the university professor who writes texts which frequently are not in tune with the needs of the two-year college.

The challenge is somewhat awesome but not insurmountable. With determination and persistance a language curriculum can be designed which will not only service the needs of the community but at the same time put the study of language back in competition with some of the other courses which are currently enjoying great popularity.

5. SUMMARY OF SMALL GROUP DISCUSSIONS ON CURRICULUM

Edited by LOUISE H. ALLEN

The three groups addressed themselves to a number of topics, chief among them being articulation with senior institutions, attracting and keeping students, and non-traditional types of courses.

1) ARTICULATION WITH SENIOR INSTITUTIONS

A number of questions were raised about the *actual* (rather than the rumored) machinery and requirements of four-year institutions. For example, does the admissions office have jurisdiction in determining course-equivalencies, or do the several departments make such determinations? Are proficiency examinations either available to or required of two-year college graduates? If the two-year graduate's proficiency score indicates a level of achievement unacceptable to the transfer college, is he required to take additional course work in foreign languages?

Are the requirements of transfer institutions more or less parallel statewide, or do they vary? What is the level of acceptability at the four-year college of non-traditional courses given in the community college? What is the role of state boards in articulation and determining equivalencies? How many community college graduates continue foreign language study at the senior college? How good are follow-up information and feedback on graduates that are available to the two-year college? Is the two-year college completely free to make its own placement in foreign language courses of its students, or does the student run the risk of having his college credit reduced by the transfer college if it is interpreted as duplication of his high school credit?

The representatives of universities indicated that determination of course-equivalencies is rather generally in the hands of departments rather than of admissions officers, but that the latter are often called upon to make interpretations applicable to specific cases from the general guidelines provided by the departments. They also pointed out that in many cases a particular foreign language requirement is imposed by an agency outside the language departments--namely, the college or school or department to which the student makes application, which may not be the administrative unit in which languages are taught. Boards of governance are now rather generally guided by university practice and recommendations; but the present wide divergence of practices among universities in the state may lead in time to more state participation in evaluation of courses and determination of equivalencies.

Several of the university professors
felt that their departments were unnecessar-
ily inflexible in the demands they made of
two-year college graduates with reference to
mastery of particular types of material.
Responding to questions about the fate at the
universities of a student who had, for example, learned the Spanish terminology for the
parts and repair of an automobile engine, one
professor said, "We have to begin to bend and
open up on this question, to make it possible
to recognize the work done at the two-year
institutions...[This] has to come about."
Another suggested, "If the junior college is
going to offer a new type of course that
hasn't been offered before, they should write
to the department and tell them what it is.
Then the department writes a note to admissions and says this course is acceptable for
whatever credit." The same professor added,
"We have to find a way not to penalize the
junior college student because his training
has not been in the same mold that our training has been." Such statements clearly offer
hope for a closer working relationship and
better mutual understanding than has previously existed between two-year and four-year
foreign language departments. However, the
Conference participants agreed that only a
beginning had been made, and that the matter
of course-equivalency determination and
assignment of credit is definitely in need of
further cooperative study and work.

Another piece of unfinished business
concerns the use of standardized tests for
credit and/or placement at the transfer
institution. Agreement was general that the
tests offer an advantage to the student who
has pursued a traditional course and a parallel disadvantage to the student who has

learned a specialized vocabulary or a regional or non-standard form of the language, however valid his purpose in doing so may have
been. But participants did not agree on the
utility of such tests for placing the student
transferring from one college to another;
some thought that they should be abolished,
some that they should be standardized state-
wide, and others that they should be made
available to community college graduates as
well as to entering freshmen. Consensus
existed on the point that tests should be
used to the *advantage* of the student, and
not to his disadvantage; but participants
felt strongly that considerably more study
and discussion are necessary for determining
how to accomplish this commendable objective.
One group's reporter neatly summed up the
dilemma: "We agreed that we must have some
kind of diagnostic test to place the student
where he ought to be, but how credit could
or should be handled was the question on
which we closed."

Several substantive suggestions for
meeting these dilemmas were made.

One was the assignment by the senior
institution of "x-credit." This is done now
in some states, and amounts to giving the
community college transfer student hours of
credit according to his transcript, but not
assigning them as fulfillment of any specific
requirement for a degree. Thus, the student
who has five hours' credit for Spanish automobile repair or French cuisine at the two-
year college might receive five hours' general education credit toward graduation from
the university without necessarily being
granted parallel satisfaction of five hours
of the language requirement. Consensus

seemed to be that this would be an improvement over no credit, but that it still would not completely free the two-year college to build its own curriculum according to its perceptions of the needs of its students.

Another suggestion was for the two-year college to grant variable credit to students in the same class, say, from zero to six or eight hours. Such credit would reflect the actual accomplishment of the individual student, and might or might not be accompanied by quality grades (A, B, C, etc.) At least one community college in the state is now considering this approach in foreign languages, and others have variable credit in learning laboratories and developmental programs. The increasing trend toward individualized packets (modules) of instruction seems likely to facilitate the variable credit system. Participants felt that such credit might reflect much more realistically than the usual lock-step credit system the true level of achievement of the student and make transfer evaluation both easier and more accurate than the traditional approach.

Discussion of feedback information to the two-year college on transfer students brought out the fact that it is difficult to trace the progress of such students at the university, particularly after the first term. The reason for this is that transfer students, once established at the senior institution, are counted in statistics simply as "continuing" students there. Thus the burden of follow-up devolves on direct contact by the two-year college with its graduates, a procedure complicated by changes of address, non-return of questionnaires, etc. Participants felt that cooperative efforts between the pre- and post-transfer colleges would be

helpful here, too. While it appears that
relatively few community college graduates
continue foreign language study as majors or
minors, some do transfer before completion
of the senior institution's requirement, and
reliable information about their progress is
important.

Procedures for handling the student who
had studied a foreign language in high school
and then been placed by the two-year college
in its FL program seem to be well routinized.
A letter from the two-year college to the
transfer institution simply explaining the
placement made seems to suffice in most cases,
and the student's college credit is generally
validated.

Finally, members of the Conference felt
strongly that continued common discussion of
the transfer problem between two-year and
senior institutions was essential, and might
well lead to specific definitions of levels
of mastery and objectives of courses. Hope
was expressed that such agreements, in turn,
would receive a favorable ear from state
boards and accrediting agencies, and thus
remove some of the present misunderstandings
and obstacles to experimentation at the
community college.

2) ATTRACTING AND KEEPING STUDENTS

In a period of declining enrollments and
active resistance to foreign language requirements, participants felt it imperative to
examine the *appeal* of foreign language
courses, both to the entering student and to
the continuing student.

Questions considered included the following:

How can students be brought to the FL
classroom in the first place? How great a
problem is attrition after a term or two?
How can foreign speakers in the community
help? Do non-credit courses and courses in
literature in translation interest students,
current or prospective, in foreign language
courses?

Several groups discussed effective public
relations materials, and pointed out that
attractive brochures, newspaper advertise-
ments, and spot announcements on radio and
television are helpful, particularly if they
include information about registration by
mail or telephone. Visitation to high
schools and community groups by instructors
and/or currently enrolled students are in-
valuable. Members of the Conference agreed
that public relations materials should be as
detailed and as eye-catching as possible,
particularly for new offerings. One college
publishes an annual tabloid section in local
newspapers, describing behavioral objectives,
teaching methods and class activities for
each offering, with pictures of classes in
action and comments from students. Those
using radio announcements strive for catchy
phrasing, and it was agreed that attractive
visuals are essential for television publicity. Colleges offering non-credit community service courses often emphasize these
in their public relations materials, and
sometimes find that students originally
attracted to these courses will eventually
move into the credit courses.

Attrition is a wide-spread problem, and
some colleges reported that "we're really
turning into a 101 department"; that is,
students enroll in the beginning course but
drop out after the first term. Remedies

suggested for meeting this problem included variable credit and individualized instruction, since lack of study time and consequent "falling behind the class" is often a reason for dropping language study.

There was discussion of textbooks and materials available in the present market, also, and the general feeling was expressed that two-year college foreign language teachers should consider designing and preparing their own books and audio-visual aids. Representatives of at least two publishing companies warmly encouraged this suggestion, noting that specialized junior college materials in English and other disciplines are being well accepted for adoption.

A number of positive factors for attracting and keeping students were cited. These included presence in the community of foreign speakers, who are both potential guest speakers and performers and potential students in literacy and literature courses and bilingual programs; one group's reporter noted that "schools with large ethnic populations seem to have no real trouble" in attracting students to the study of the language of the ethnic group. Another group spoke of the "culture contrast" technique as an effective one, sharpening the student's awareness of his own American culture by comparing its features with those of the target language. An obvious plus is the dynamic, vital teacher whom two-year colleges seek out; one group spoke of "a kind of personality cult" in this connection--the spreading of the word that certain instructors are effective, dedicated, charming, etc., in short "good teachers." While difficult to foster and disseminate, this is of course the very best kind of "advertising."

3) NON-TRADITIONAL COURSES

Many colleges offer community service courses for no credit; these serve would-be travelers, ethnic groups seeking literacy in their native tongue or study of their native literature, vocational-technical students with need for bilingual skills, and groups simply interested in one or another aspect of a foreign culture. Participants from outside Illinois were dismayed that virtually all of these courses are non-credit, and they recommended that Illinois colleges "somehow try to get the community service programs into the credit structure."

Foreign language instructors are also involved in humanities and literature courses in some colleges. These offer the opportunity to introduce students to foreign cultures and are sometimes sufficiently intriguing to generate later enrollment in FL courses. Consensus seemed to be that the development and encouragement of such courses is healthy for foreign language programs and should be pursued.

There was agreement, too, that opportunities for working with English as a second language and with Americanization programs should be investigated by FL faculties, particularly in areas with large ethnic populations. Familiarity with the native language and culture on the part of the instructor is helpful (if not essential) in classes in these materials, and a team-teaching approach with persons trained in TESL should produce an unusually effective program.

82

SUMMARY

The discussion groups addressed themselves earnestly to better ways of doing what
FL teachers have always done -instructing
students in the language and occasionally in
its literature- and of relating instruction
to the particular needs of individual students and groups of students to the maximum
degree possible. Design of curriculum is
obviously an important aspect of this, and
it was generally agreed that the two-year
college needs a somewhat unorthodox curriculum. Problems of articulation and budgeting, unavailability of appropriate textbooks
and materials, and hesitancy on the part of
local and state boards to approve innovative
courses and variable credit systems are merely obstacles to be overcome. Enthusiasm,
ideas, and collaborative effort can and
should result in dramatic new kinds of
foreign language programs, and thus answer
the question "Whither?"

6. THE APPLICATION OF TECHNOLOGY
TO THE TEACHING OF FOREIGN LANGUAGES

RICHARD T. SCANLAN
University of Illinois

It is unnecessary to point out to an experienced teacher the important supportive
role which the audio-visual media can play in
a classroom presentation. As language teachers we are challenged to take advantage of
technology wherever it can be used to improve
the quality of our teaching. As individual
teachers we need to attain and maintain a
familiarity with the capabilities of the hardware, the quality of available materials, and
the ways in which each medium can contribute
to language learning. This paper will emphasize some of the newer applications of technology to FL teaching and where appropriate
indicate sources for obtaining materials and
further information.

THE PLATO SYSTEM OF COMPUTER-ASSISTED INSTRUCTION

PLATO is a computer-based teaching system
located at the University of Illinois which

provides a means for individualizing student instruction. Teacher, computer, and students are all members of an interactive team. The teacher designs the instructional material; the computer presents the material to the students, at the same time monitoring and evaluating their performance; and the students interact with the computer, providing information on lesson effectiveness. Each student works at his own pace on material which can provide special information and help when problems arise. The teacher can easily revise instructional material to modernize or improve it. PLATO frees the teacher for special work with students which conventional teaching styles do not usually permit.

The PLATO III system presently consists of 75 terminals. Thirty-six are located on the campus of the University of Illinois in Urbana-Champaign. Thirty-nine are located at remote sites, including one in Springfield. Up to twenty of these terminals may be used by students and lesson writers at any one time.

A PLATO III terminal consists of a keyset which transmits the user's input to a central computer and a video display which can simultaneously show computer-generated information and computer-selected photographic slides to the user.

All PLATO III terminals are controlled by a single computer. The terminals share an electric slide selector and each is connected to an individual cathode ray storage tube (TV picture tube) which provides the image on the screen.

This year the PLATO IV system at the University of Illinois is beginning expansion to 4,000 terminals located within an approximate

150 mile radius of Urbana-Champaign, all
accessing a central computer via telephone
lines.

PLATO IV uses a plasma display panel in
lieu of a TV storage tube and a high-speed
individual slide selector will also be available as optional equipment for the terminal.

Time-sharing operations of authoring,
teaching, and computational modes will allow
efficient individualized use of the large
scale computer with access by students to
about 250 lessons at any one time.

Estimated costs for the new system are
35¢ to 50¢ per student per terminal hour.

The following computer-assisted FL
courses are already available on PLATO III
and will be available on PLATO IV:

    French 101 - Beginning French
    French 102 - Beginning French
    French 103 - Intermediate French
    French 104 - Intermediate French
    French 313 - French Phonetics

    Latin 101 - Beginning Latin
    Latin 102 - Beginning Latin
    Latin 103 - Intermediate Latin
    Latin 104 - Vergil's *Aeneid*
    Latin 113 - Latin Composition
    Latin 114 - Latin Composition

    Russian 101 - Beginning Russian
    Russian 121 - Beginning Russian through
                  Reading
    Russian 122 - Beginning Russian through
                  Reading

```
Spanish 101 - Beginning Spanish
              (accelerated)
Spanish 102 - Beginning Spanish
              (accelerated)
Spanish 103 - Intermediate Spanish
```

Programs are planned and a few lessons developed for German and Italian. Most of the lessons may be divided into segments and adapted to flexible scheduling and credit.

Furth information may be obtained from Professor M.K.Myers, 362 Engineering Research Laboratory, University of Illinois, Urbana 61801 or Professor R.T.Scanlan, 4072 Foreign Languages Building, University of Illinois, Urbana 61801.

TELEVISION

Recent studies have established that children see at least 4,000 hours of television by the time they enter kindergarten and that exposure continues at a daily rate of from two to five hours throughout elementary and secondary school. Clearly our students are accustomed to this medium and feel at home with it. The three items of equipment necessary for effective use of TV in the FL classroom are available in most schools and colleges: a television camera, a monitor, and a video-tape recorder. If a system for closed-circuit relay is also available all the better. Three uses of the medium should be pointed out:

1) Prerecorded videotapes. There are several sources for such tapes:
a) a library of 1300 free-loan 16 mm sound films has been transferred to one-inch tape. Information may be obtained from Modern Talking Picture Service, 1212 Avenue of the Americas, New York, NY 10036;

b) many public television programs are available from KCET ETV Channel 28, Community Television of Southern California, 1313 North Vine Street, Los Angeles, California 90028;

c) another source of information about prerecorded tapes is Ampex Tape Exchange, Ampex Corporation, 2201 Trent Avenue, Elk Grove Village, Illinois 60007;

d) recent telecourses which have been developed are listed in ETV *Newsletter*, C.S. Tepfer Publishing Corporation, 140 Main Street, Ridgefield, Connecticut 06877.

2) "Homemade" videotapes. Videotapes can be made in the classroom: conversational situations can be simulated (or a native speaker can be interviewed and the tape used in the classroom), scenes from plays or skits can be presented (complete with commercials in the FL), or simple drills can be recorded. The basic elements of language learning can be emphasized in any of these activities and the student will receive immediate reinforcement. Because he is working with a medium to which he has been widely exposed and because he can both see and hear himself, the videotape recording is likely to have more impact upon the student than just a sound recording. Most of the video-recorders are no more difficult to use than tape-recorders, and they provide the same flexibility in editing, dubbing and re-use of tapes. For those without the necessary hardware, the use for language practice of television game show formats can add greater variety and interest to the FL classroom.

3) "Mini-institutes" for teachers can be videotaped and then circulated among the junior colleges in the state. Each of the taped institutes would run approximately sixty minutes and could emphasize a particular theme or idea applicable to FL teaching in general

or to problem areas in a given language.
Participants could be chosen from the junior
colleges or from other colleges and universities throughout the state as appropriate.
Possible topics for such institutes might be:
problems in teaching FL's to special interest
groups such as social workers or policemen;
suggestions for and demonstrations of imaginative drill and practice routines; games in
the FL classroom; the teaching of culture;
review of current FL texts; demonstration of
the effective use of audio-visual equipment;
description and demonstration of successful
FL programs in various junior colleges
throughout the state. Some of the topics
might be effectively presented on the state-
wide confernce telephone system available in
the Division of Extension at the University
of Illinois, but most require a visual component lacking in that system.

FILMS

There are three uses of film which I wish
to emphasize in this report.

1) Feature films. There are many companies which distribute recent feature films
for showing in educational institutions. The
cost for rental of these films varies considerably, but most films can be rented at a
cost of from $25 to $75. Such films are
enormously valuable in highlighting the cultural component of FL study but may also be
helpful in basic language study when the dialogue is in the target language. In the
latter case it is necessary to do fairly extensive preparation for the film, and it is
valuable to have a projector which allows for
stopping and rerunning while the film is in
progress. Film is another medium in which our
students feel at home and I cannot over-empha-
size its usefulness (especially feature films)

as a supplement to FL instruction. Often, where money is not available for film rental, the students themselves will be willing to pay the cost. Since feature films often run longer than class period, it may be necessary to show them on successive days or to arrange a special time for presentation. A list of some of the feature film distributors follows. Each of these companies will send a free catalogue upon request.

- a) Audio Film Center, 2138 East 75th St., Chicago 60649
- b) Brandon Films, 221 West 57th St., New york City 10019
- c) Contemporary Films, 828 Custer Avenue, Evanston 60202
- d) Films Incorporated, 4420 Oakton Street, Skokie 60076
- e) Institutional Cinema Service, Inc., 67 East Madison, Chicago 60603
- f) Modern Talking Picture Service, 1212 Avenue of the Americas, New York 10036 (*Free* loan of over 1300 films)
- g) Twyman Films, P.O. Box 605, Dayton, Ohio 45401

2) Eight mm films. New cameras and projectors have made the taking and showing of smaller size motion picture film much easier. It is a rare class where there are not some students who have access to a camera for taking eight or "super eight" size film. Most of the inexpensive cameras of this type shoot silent film, and the sound (where important) must be supplied through a tape-recorder or through a live commentary as the film is being shown. Many projects using this medium suggest themselves to the imaginative teacher. A scene or situation or skit can be filmed by one team of students while another group, after seeing the film, must

supply what they feel to be the appropriate
dialogue or narrative in the FL. Or the
same scene can be shown to the class as a
whole for their "live" description in the FL.
Total productions (involving both film and
sound) can be assigned to various members of
the class. Films of this sort can also be
made available for individual study in the
"learning resource center" or carrels.
Small size films have also been used by
teachers to produce "single concept" film
loops in which a delimited idea is explored
in depth on a 50 foot reel. The student
studying alone can view the films as many
times as necessary until he understands the
concept. Preparation of such "loops" is
quite time consuming as no step, however
minor, can be left out in the exploration of
the concept.

3) Educational films. Thousands of excellent films are available from Audio-Visual
Aids, University of Illinois, 1325 Oak Street,
Champaign 61820, at inexpensive rental rates.
A complete catalogue of all films available
from this source is usually found in the
office of the Audio-Visual Director of any
given junior college, or it may be ordered
at a cost of $3. A free catalogue of films
selected for their appropriateness to FL instruction may be obtained by writing to the
above address. Teachers from junior colleges
in Chicago (which has its own educational
film agency) may still want to examine the
catalogue for titles. A critique of French
films available may be obtained from Sandra
Savignon, Department of French, 2090 FLB,
University of Illinois, Urbana 61801; a critique of German listings from Vincent Dell'
Orto, Department of German, 3072 FLB.

TRANSPARENCIES

Images that have been written, drawn, or printed on transparent material can be shown on an overhead projector. Despite increased availability of the machine as a teaching tool, many language teachers are still unfamiliar with it. The overhear projector provides many technological advantages: (1) it is simple to operate; (2) it requires little maintenance; (3) it can be used in a lighted room without drawing the shades; (4) the teacher faces the class while using the machine; (5) materials which would ordinarily be written on the blackboard can be copied on a transparency in advance, thus making more efficient use of classroom time; (6) the image can be projected onto a wall, a screen, or the blackboard; (7) colors can be used to highlight certain features of the presentation; (8) a mask (a layer of opaque material placed over the transparency) which blocks out part of the image can be used when the teacher wishes to emphasize a single point at a time; (9) an overlay technique can be used in which one transparency is placed on top of another, e.g., a student composition is copied onto one transparency and then the teacher's corrections on a second transparency are placed over the original sheet; (10) any material with carbon content can be copied with a thermofax machine directly onto a transparency and shown on the overhead projector. Sources for commercially prepared transparencies are available from the MLA. One of the larger distributors is: Educational Audio-Visual, Inc., Pleasantville, New York 10570. A free catalogue will be sent upon request. In general, however, the overhead projector is used far more often to present homemade materials than those from commercial sources. Where it is used effectively, it becomes a part of the day to day operation of the class and is more essential to FL instruction than a blackboard.

SLIDES

Thirty-five mm slides can be a useful adjunct to the FL classroom, especially in emphasizing the cultural component. A complete source list for slides can be obtained from the MLA. Some of the leading distributors from whom catalogues may be requested are:

a) American Library Color Slide Co., 305 East 45th Street, New York, NY 10017
b) Budek Films and Slides, inc., P.O. Box 307, Santa Barbara, Cal. 93102
c) Roloc, Box 1715, Washington, DC 20013
d) Wolfe Worldwide Films, 1657 Sautelle Blvd., Los Angeles, C

Multi-media presentation in which the showing of slides is coordinated with a taped narrative and music can be very effective. It is also possible (and interesting) to make one's own slides to illustrate a story to be narrated or as a series for which students invent their own narrative or give their own commentary. Students may be encouraged to make their own sets (from ordinary, everyday scenes, e.g., children at play, people in the street) and to prepare a narrative in the FL to accompany it. The narrative can be perfected and taped to add to a library of such slide/commentary series.

Since slide reproductions are often expensive (25¢ to $1 per slide), two alternatives must be suggested. It is possible to make one's own slides from pictures in books and magazines (if not from the original locales themselves), although this process can be quite technical. Second, pictures from books and magazines or on prints can be shown with an opaque projector. This is clearly an inferior form of presentation since movement from one picture to another is often awkward and time consuming, but it is still better than no supplement of this type at all.

FILM-STRIPS

Film-strips offer the teacher the same kind of visual presentation as do slides and have the advantage that they are much less expensive. The disadvantage is that the order of presentation is predetermined by the producer of the film and may often contain items which the teacher believes are not pertinent to the study at hand. Some of the leading distributors of film-strips are:

a) Encyclopedia Britannica Educational Corp., 425 Michigan Avenue, Chicago 60611
b) Life Film-strips, 9 Rockefeller Plaza, New York, NY 10020
c) Library Film-strip Center, 3033 Aloma, Wichita, Kansas 67211
d) Pathescope Educational Films, 71 Weyman Avenue, New Rochelle, NY 10802

Other sources may be obtained from the MLA.

It is also possible to make one's own film-strips. Successful slide series prepared by the students (described under V above) can be combined into filmstrips (less expensive than slides) for future use.

RECORDS

The impact which the music of a foreign
country can have upon the student's understanding of a foreign culture should not be
underestimated. I mean here not just music
appreciation, but the learning of foreign
songs and dances. Folk, popular, and class-
ical music can all be used as offering an
insight into the foreign culture, and indeed
the lyrics for such music can be an intrinsic
part of basic language study. A proposed
course in the German Department at the University of Illinois, for example, will concentrate on the study of German opera librettos. Many students enjoy learning various
folk-dances of the foreign country, and many
records are available for this kind of activity. Also available are dramatic readings
by professional actors of literary selections
in various foreign languages. Materials of
this type can also enrich the classroom experience.

AUDIOTAPES

If there is an application of the audio-
visual media to teaching with which almost
all FL instructors have had experience, it is
with the use of audiotapes. It is through
tapes that the lesson has best been learned
that the medium is *not* the message, that content and quality are the important factors in
any classroom supplement. It is perhaps unnecessary to point out that the most effective
use of audiotapes occurs when their content is
closely coordinated with classroom work. It
seems best, if there is time, for the teacher
to make as many of his own tapes as possible.
Whether the student is responding as part of
a group to a recorder controlled by the teacher or whether he works individually in a classroom station, a study carrel, or a language

laboratory, the material on the tape must appeal to the student intellectually and emotionally and possess the pacing and variety which any competent classroom presentation would. The material for such tapes is not necessarily worked out from the base by the teacher but may consist of a variety of items dubbed from different sources to make an interesting lesson appropriate to the current work which the students are learning. An interesting variation of the basic language laboratory concept is quite popular with students at the University of Illinois. Telephone lines are made available for classes of those teachers who request them. Recorded programs can thus be accessed by the student at any time through the telephone. The French Department uses this system to make available daily French newscasts taped from a shortwave radio and readings of poetry and plays being studied.

I shall conclude this report with a brief description of the *new look* in a FL laboratory at the University of Illinois. This laboratory will soon take concrete form in the Foreign Languages Building. A student station will have the following components: a plasma screen for displaying computer generated material (PLATO) and on which a computer controlled slide selector will project color or black and white slides, speakers or earhones for computer controlled random-access audio material, a key-set by which the student presents graphic responses to problems presented, and a microphone through which he gives oral responses. To this may be added a TV monitor for displaying color videotapes or a "super eight" motion picture projector. The challenge which such technological sophistication presents to the teacher is clear, but the results in student motivation and learning could be equally impressive.

Whether we work in such a laboratory or not, the future points to increasing use of the media by teachers in all disciplines.

7. PREPARATION OF FOREIGN LANGUAGE TEACHERS FOR THE JUNIOR-COMMUNITY COLLEGE

SANDRA J. SAVIGNON
University of Illinois

A young FL teacher on her first teaching assignment came back to the halls of the Big U wanting, she said, to inquire about graduate school. I asked her how her teaching was going. "Dreadful" was the answer. She went on to explain that she was teaching in a small rural community in downstate Illinois. "Because I couldn't find anything else. The kids of Narrawong are so narrow-minded. Nobody really wants to learn and it doesn't do any good to flunk them. They aren't concerned about getting into college. Nobody ever leaves Narrawong!" As our discussion continued, it was clear that the teacher felt she was working in intolerable circumstances and would get out as soon as she could, hopefully to the cushy refuge--however temporary--of further graduate study.

Clearly, her university training had not prepared this young teacher for what she was

to find in Narrawong. More seriously, it had
reinforced a cultural bias which hindered an
authentic response to the specific context in
which she was involved. She had sufficient
insight to see that her expectations had been
inappropriate, but she didn't know where to
go from there. She realized that the commercial teaching materials she was using didn't
work, but she didn't know with what to replace them, or indeed, if any effort she
might make was worthwhile. Ultimately she
would blame her failure on the students and,
more generally, on the community.

The reaction of this young teacher is repeated every year. There are dozens of Nar-
rawongs in the State of Illinois. While this
particular incident relates specifically to
a rural high school context, the parallel
with FL learning in the junior and community
colleges is apparent. FL teachers in these
colleges are frequently faced with students
who do not have the cultural perspective of
students enrolled in a four-year institution.
Junior college students are not always concerned with articulation toward advanced level courses at a senior college, and they have
real and immediate needs which may not be
readily apparent to an insensitive FL teacher
from a different socio-cultural background.

It would be self-delusion for us to suggest that the remedy to this young teacher's
unpreparedness lies where she think it *auto-
matically* lies: in continued study--this
time on the graduate level. According to the
testimony of at least some teachers who have
traveled this path, the most valuable component of their graduate training appears to
have been *not* the additional course work, but
the incidental experience they gained as a
teaching assistant in the University FL department. These same teachers go on to note,

however, that even this experience was finally
inappropriate, leading them to false expectations in terms of student interests and abilities in the high school or community college
where they would teach.

Must not our professional heads as well
as our human hearts go out to this young woman? As we begin our discussion of teacher
training for foreign languages in junior-
community colleges we need to keep in mind
the following characteristics of the colleges
which, to some extent, are not unlike those
of many secondary schools. First, the junior-community college is *people-oriented.*[1]
There is more concern with the needs of the
individual student than at most four year institutions. The teacher in the junior-community college must be prepared to spend many
hours outside the classroom tutoring and
counseling students who range in age from 18
to 80 and who come from a wide variety of
socio-cultural backgrounds. Secondly, the
junior-community college is *community-oriented*. Whereas the four-year institution most
often exists as a "microcosm" with no particular ties to the immediate enviroment in
which it finds itself, the junior-community
college emerges as a result of the efforts of
the community. It has as its *raison d'etre*
the particular needs and concerns of that
community. Teachers must, therefore, be able
to evaluate these needs and concerns and be
prepared to implement programs which satisfy
them.

This brings us to a third characteristic
of the junior-community college which bears
directly on FL offerings: it is broad in its
cultural orientation. Answering the call for
diversity in curriculum planning and development requires on the part of the FL teacher a
linguistic and cultural background that is

100

not currently provided by the typical Language plus Literature program of most undergraduate and graduate teacher training programs. While there are many students who anticipate transfer to a four-year institution and who enroll in a FL program to satisfy entrance requirements, the majority of these students do not pursue their FL study beyond what is in most cases a required two-year sequence. Other students are not concerned with requirements *per se* but look to FL study to satisfy a variety of personal or professional needs: Puerto Ricans seeking secretarial jobs using their native language, residents of a rural Amish community interested in exploring their German heritage, professionals who want to brush up on their spoken French before a business trip to Paris. The needs vary from one community to another. The concerns of an inner-city community are not the same as those of a rural community. Junior-community colleges which prepare large numbers of students for transfer to four-year institutions have different curricular requirements than those whose emphasis is primarily technical-vocational training.

What then are the special requirements of a training program which will equip the teacher to successfully face the challenge of FL teaching in the community college? What kinds of in-service programs need to be created to help the teacher who is already on the job? The three characteristics of junior-community colleges outlined above provide a framework within which we can now address ourselves to these and other questions which may arise from our discussions, leading us to an examination of several prototypes for pre-service and in-service training of the community college FL teacher.

A. PERSONAL-ORIENTATION OF THE COMMUNITY
COLLEGE FL TEACHER. The faculty evaluation
form of a large community college in Illinois
lists *Concern for Students* as one of the four
criteria used in determining the tenure and
advancement of its teaching staff. "The
programs and services of the College are designed to provide the greatest practicable
degree of faculty attention to each student.
The development of students and their personal improvement shall be the foremost concern of the faculty and staff."[2] A division
chairman at this same institution remarked
that in her experience former members of the
clergy and persons with Peace Corps experience were among their finest teachers. The
question which this insight raises is whether
an integrative approach to teaching in terms
of a commitment to students' needs *outside*
as well as within a particular area of study
is one that can be fostered by specialized
training, and if so, what kind? Or are we
dealing with inherent characteristics which
prompt an individual toward various types
of service careers? If this is the case
are there means of assessing these characteristics prior to admitting a candidate to the
training program? If we accept the premise
that successful teaching is a combination of
both art and science, what specific courses
are most valuable in preparing the already
integratively oriented teacher or teacher-
trainee for his work with community college
students of the diversity we have noted? Are
there already existent courses in psychology,
counseling and guidance which are appropriate?
What new courses need to be developed? Who
is best qualified to teach them?

B. COMMUNITY ORIENTATION OF THE COMMUNI-
TY COLLEGE FL TEACHER. We have emphasized
the need for responsiveness on the part of the
community college teacher to the needs of a

102

community with which he may not have had
prior experience. This responsiveness would
also encompass an ability to enlist the aid
of local resource persons in designing and
implementing specialized courses: street
Spanish for social workers, business Polish
for native speakers, an exploration of the
ethnic diversity of the community, and so on.
Again, what kinds of courses are needed and
who should teach them? Can a course such as
*Problems of Junior Colleges in Urban and
Rural Areas* provide meaningful input? Can
on-the-spot practice in community relations
be provided as part of a teaching internship?
If so, how?

C. CULTURAL ORIENTATION OF THE COMMUNITY
COLLEGE FL TEACHER. The need for diversified,
community-oriented FL offerings brings us to
the specialized training required of the community college FL teacher. Foremost among
these requirements, stressed repeatedly by
community college personnel, is a broad *linguistic* and *cultural* background. The teacher needs to be unquestionably fluent in the
language he is teaching and must have had
first-hand experience in the culture of a
community, country or countries where the
language is spoken. The holder of a traditional doctoral degree in Language and Literature does not usually meet these requirements. In the words of one administrator,
"I would rather hire the man who has lived
with the people and within the language, than
the man who wrote the footnotes."[3] In the
familiar short-hand of our curriculum debates,
the community college FL teacher must be concerned with culture with a small-c far more
than with the capital-C or High Culture of
the typical four-year college curriculum in
our field. A new curriculum of *Area Studies*
developed within the FL department and exploring the social, political and historical

103

identity of that particular language group,
would offer a meaningful alternative to the
literary period and genre courses which now
prevail. With this kind of background the
teacher will be ready to illustrate the "hows"
and "whys" of everyday life and thought in the
foreign culture, providing students with a
unique opportunity for experiencing cultural
diversity.[4]

Of equal importance for the community college FL teacher is a background in the *psychological and linguistic foundations of second-
language acquisition*. The community college
enjoys relative autonomy in terms of curriculum design, giving it exciting potential as
a field for experimentation with new approaches to teaching and to course design. Yet many
teachers, formed by the literary mandarinate
of university FL departments, lack sufficient
preparation and even respect for the role of
the FL specialist. If teachers are given the
opportunity to develop a professional enthusiasm for methodology and an understanding of
its theoretical underpinnings, the community
college could become a proving ground for innovative ideas in FL and, in turn, provide
valuable feedback to more tradition-bound
high schools and senior colleges. Here, for
example, the current interest in team-teaching
might find unique application, for the community can provide members of teaching teams not
only from "certified" teachers but for appropriate content portions of a given course,
living models from the community itself:
secretaries, mechanics, etc.

A third focus of the specialized training
of the FL teacher is in the use of *media*.
Film, radio, television and, in particular,
computer programs promise glamorous new dimensions in FL instruction. The community college teacher needs to keep abreast of develop-

ments, needs to know where to obtain materials and to have the technical know-how to use them. But owning and being able to operate the hardware are not enough: witness the language laboratories lying vacant and in disrepair across the land. What use can be made of television and radio, including short-wave radio broadcasts? Which movies are most likely to correspond to student interests? And what of computer-assisted programs which offer the possibility for broader implementation of individualized programs by freeing the teacher from some of the didactics of FL learning. *But the nature of what goes with such programs is crucial to the success of the program.* It is up to the well-trained and experienced classroom teacher to learn what the computer can do best with FL instruction. Then, leaving drills and other formal exercises to the machine, the *human* teacher is ready to do what he alone can do: provide the opportunity for *real language* use by interacting with his students in *authentic,* communicative exchanges. In so doing, he will realize his full potential as the people-oriented, community oriented specialist in a foreign language and culture that he was trained to be.

The foregoing discussion of the needs of the FL community college teacher suggests a training program which might resemble the following prototype on the M.A. or M.A.T. level, presupposing a year of study abroad as part of the undergraduate major.

HOURS	COURSE DESCRIPTION
4	FL curriculum development and the use of media
12-16	Area Studies (contemporary culture, history, arts, cinema, comparative culture, world influence of a language group, etc.)

```
                  of a language group, etc.)
4-8       Language skills (radio newscasts,
               business Spanish, French, etc.,
               popular journals, etc., possibly
               coordinated with an Area Studies
               offering)
          Comprehensive Test of Oral Compe-
               tence
4         Second-language acquisition:  a
               psycholinguistic analysis
4         Psychology and sociology of the
___            community college student
32  hours total plus an Internship in a
    community college
```

It is assumed that all but perhaps a
course in the psychology and sociology of the
community college student would be specialized
or joint offerings of the FL departments involved.

In evaluating and elaborating this and
other prototypes which emerge from our discussions we will need to formulate answers to
the following questions.

1) What innovations, if any, are needed
in traditional undergraduate teacher training programs to prepare students for a Master's level program such as the one outlined?

2) What provisions need to be made for
persons lacking first-hand experience in the
culture of the language they are teaching or
are preparing to teach?

3) How feasible is an internship program
in Illinois?

4) Are the community colleges interested?
Who should supervise the trainee, the senior
institution, the community college, or both?

5) Is there an interest on the part of community college FL teachers and supervisory personnel in a short term (two to four week) summer in-service institute? If so, what form should it take?

6) Is there a market in the community colleges for the doctoral candidate specializing in language teaching, or are programs for community college FL teachers best limited to the M.A. level? If a doctoral level program is recommended, what components should it include?

7) In formulating training programs, need we think in terms of separate degrees, supposedly distinguishing between research-oriented (M.A., Ph.D.) and teaching-oriented candidates (M.A.T., D.A.)? Or does a *multi-track graduate program* allow for the best quality control, assuming that all graduate degree candidates are preparing for teaching or teaching-related careers and that research can take many forms, including experiments in language acquisition and curriculum design as well as literary criticism?

In providing answers to these questions we will go a long way toward describing workable training programs which will help to create and maintain the kinds of FL offerings which the students (and teachers) in our community colleges want and deserve.

NOTES

1. Louise H. Allen has used the terms
   people-oriented and *community-oriented*
   to describe the community college in
   "The Colleges of the 80's--or Where
   the Action Is," paper read at the ACTFL
   Conference, Chicago, Nov.1971. See above.
2. Faculty Evaluation Form, Parkland Col-
   Lege, Champaign, Illinois, 1972.
3. Normal D. Arbaiza in "The Training and
   Orientation of Foreign Language Teachers
   in the Junior Colleges: A Conference
   Report," *ADFL Bulletin*, III,No.1,Sept.,
   1971,p.46.
4. Robert J. Nelson has proposed such a program in French, "A Modern Curriculum in
   French Studies." in *French Language Education: The Teaching of Culture in the
   Classroom*, eds. C.Jay and P. Castle
   (Springfield, Illinois: Office of the
   Superintendent of Public Instruction,
   1971),pp.64-74.

7.   PREPARATION OF FOREIGN LANGUAGE TEACHERS
     FOR THE JUNIOR-COMMUNITY COLLEGE: A RESPONSE

SUSAN E. KARR
University of Washington

Early in her paper Professor Savignon charac-
terizes the community college as being com-
munity- and people-oriented. Theoretically
and ideally this is quite true. In reality,
however, the community college is all too often university-oriented, a fact which comes
out again and again in discussions with
teachers and administrators connected with
the two year schools.

University orientation can take many
forms. For example, in some states the two-
year schools have to have courses approved by
the four-year schools before the former can
offer such courses for credit. Such university orientation, whether voluntary or imposed, can mean disaster for the two-year
school. Let me illustrate what I mean.

Currently there is no proficiency requirement in foreign languages in the Wash-

109

ington State System of Higher Education. The
University of Washington, the largest institution in the state, dropped its proficiency
requirement in 1969, choosing only to retain
a two-quarter deficiency requirement, which
brought it closer to the position the other
public four-year schools in Washington have
taken on this matter. Earlier this year I
attempted to get in touch with foreign language personnel at all of the state's two-
year schools by questionnaire and telephone.
I was successful in about eighty percent of
the cases.

One question I asked concerned enrollment,
as of Winter Quarter 1972, in the various
languages that the school offered. The results were quite interesting. At one of the
more "academic" community colleges (i.e., one
with a high percentage of transfer students)
it was reported that there were 90 students
enrolled in the first-year program in German,
and 15 enrolled in the second-year program.
At one of the more "non-academic" community
colleges, the ratio between first- and second-
year enrollments, again in German, was 17 to
none. The major reasons for such a typical
disparity between first- and second-year enrollments seem to be the deficiency requirement at the University of Washington and the
varying foreign language requirements of majors in specific departments. As one of
those who responded to my questionnaire expressed it: "The majority of our foreign
language students are filling requirements of
four-year institutions. Our courses are designed to parallel those of the four-year
schools."

This particular school, as well as others
with which I have been in contact, has not
yet realized that a primary university-orien-
tation can mean disaster. As universities

drop or modify their requirements, enrollments seem to drop at the two-year schools
in the related studies. As enrollments drop,
offerings are cut. As offerings are cut,
teachers are let go. Unless this chain of
cause and effect is broken, there may soon
not be foreign language programs in the community colleges at all.

What can be done to combat such university orientation?

1) The two-year schools must somehow become more autonomous. As far as the state
of Illinois goes, now is the time to push for
acceptance and implementation of the guidelines outlined by Professor Ernest Anderson,
the University of Illinois Coordinator of
Articulation with Junior Colleges. Further,
the possibility of instituting so-called "X-
credit" for such things as project courses
and certain community service programs
should be investigated.

2) Someone has to start training foreign
language teachers with priorities other than
those of the four-year schools, which may
mean priorities other than the study of literature. The problem is who should or who
could become involved in such training programs. Where are the foreign language educators who can offer course work and learning experiences in which literature takes
second place behind, say, area studies,
ethnic awareness, or psycholinguistics?

3) As for the psychology and sociology
of the community college student, where are
the educators who can instill a concern for
students? In many cases these people are not
to be found in traditional language departments, which are often long on literary critics and scholars and short on educators.

Perhaps the answer to this question of who should become involved with training teachers for the two-year schools lies in a well-administered cooperative arrangement between a foreign language department at a large university and related departments at that university, such as linguistics, psychology, sociology, anthropology, and higher education, and a two-year college or school district.

Now, even if such cooperation between departments and individuals could be achieved, difficulties would still remain. One major problem is obvious: who is going to hire the newly trained teachers. Returning to my survey for a moment, one question which I posed was: "Do you believe there should be programs to train foreign language teachers for the two-year schools?" One-third of those who responded said "no". The most prevalent reason given by those opposed to training programs was that the two-year schools already have such an overabundance of candidates to choose from that to establish new programs to train yet more teachers would border on lunacy.

Perhaps the situation I describe here is a local one, confined to the state of Washington. If, however, it represents a national trend, or worse, a national fact, then perhaps we should think further before trying to set up training programs to turn out yet more new teachers. In this connection I would like to suggest a possible alternative to Professor Savignon's pre-service teacher-training proposal. The curriculum she presents is good--it is broad and flexible. Why couldn't it be offered as in-service, rather than pre-service, training? That is, why couldn't it be offered to those who already teach foreign languages at the communi-

ty college level? As an in-service M.A. or
M.A.T. program, it would give those teaching
in the two-year schools the opportunity to
obtain (re)training in areas such as: new
teaching methodologies, individualized instruction, options for community service,
ethnic awareness, and ways of adapting new
audio-visual aids and other technical innovations to their unique situations. Perhaps
best of all, it would give teachers the opportunity to share their frustrations and
work together to solve common problems. Such
an in-service program might improve both the
morale and the effectiveness of the community
college foreign language teacher, with the
result that foreign language programs might
be expanded, thus creating new markets.
Then, and only then, should we talk about
pre-service programs to train new teachers.

One unique feature of such an in-service
program could be the provision of an opportunity for foreign language teachers to
learn about teaching English as a foreign
language. Most two-year schools draw upon
large ethnic populations, and by offering
English to such groups can expand and diver-
sify their programs.

Let me quickly summarize what I have said.
First, I agree with Professor Savignon that
the community college should be people- and
community-oriented. The challenge facing
educators today is how to train or retrain
teachers who will make this ideal a reality.
Second, the curriculum which Professor Savignon outlines sounds very good, but I wonder which currently structured department or
administrative unit would be willing and able
to implement such a program. Finally, I challenge the idea that pre-service teacher-
training programs are the answer. I submit,
and I am not alone in this, that, given the

present imbalance between the supply of
teachers and the demand for teachers, we
should be talking about in-service, rather
than pre-service programs.

7. **SUMMARY OF FINDINGS: PREPARATION OF FOREIGN LANGUAGE TEACHERS FOR THE JUNIOR-COMMUNITY COLLEGE**

SANDRA J. SAVIGNON, University of Illinois

SUSAN E. KARR, University of Washington

VIVIAN MASTERS, Illinois Central College, East Peoria, Illinois

Conference discussions focused clearly on the inadequacy of existing university FL programs as teacher preparation for the junior-community college. Whether or not they are given a different name, degree programs must be designed which prepare community college FL teachers to meet present demands for innovation and diversification. Where articulation with FL programs at four-year institutions is a major concern, community college teachers need to push for acceptance of innovative curricula which are more responsive to the broader educational needs of today's students. (It is significant in this respect that the most interesting, most varied FL offerings in our community colleges now come under the "no credit" rubric.) Well-trained, articulate teachers are more likely to be successful in bringing new ideas into the mainstream of FL education. Those who do succeed will provide models for their colleagues at more tradition-bound institutions.

There was a consensus that initial efforts should be directed toward developing *in-service* programs for teachers who have already earned a B.A. or an M.A. degree. In-service programs for teachers already in the field (as distinguished from pre-service programs) would mark the best beginning, taking into account two significant factors in the current situation: 1) the admitted unpreparedness of community college teachers now on the job and 2) the existing imbalance between supply and demand of FL teachers on all levels. These programs should be set up for the summer months so as to make them available to community college teachers throughout the state. Summer in-service programs would have the additional important advantage of assuring the availability of staff.

Such specially designed summer programs would provide community college teachers with a meaningful opportunity to earn the additional graduate credit hours they need for professional advancement. The Ph.D. now appears in many cases to be a hindrance, rather than a help, to job candidates with no prior experience in a community college. Once on the job, however, up to 60 graduate hours may be earned for promotion in rank. In the words of one teacher, "We then take every summer or every other summer to go to Mexico, to Peru, to Spain, to Valencia... continuing with the very kinds of courses that actually add nothing. Well, they are great fun, and we need them as food for the soul, but we don't go back to the community colleges with the kinds of skills that are so desperately needed by all our people."

There was general agreement that the M.A.

program outlined in the position paper represents, both in content and proportion, the kind of preparation that is needed. Crucial to the success of such a program is the cooperation of specialists in several fields who are willing and able to begin where the community college teacher is. Teaching staff should come from university FL departments, community colleges or districts, and related disciplines (higher education, psychology, linguistics).

A course in the psychology and sociology of the community college student should be taught by a specialist from a community college. This might be a counselor who could address himself to the ethnic diversity in the student population and, where he is able, to the role of language use in self-identification and its implications for second-language acquisition.

A course in curriculum development and the use of media would ideally be a team-teaching endeavor by a university and a community college FL teacher. Their aim would be to explore together available resources and their proven and possible uses in the community college. Similarly in discussions of curriculum design, a university-community college team would provide the most effective integration of the theoretical and the practical.

A course in second-language acquisition should be taught by someone knowledgeable in psycholinguistic and sociolinguistic factors in language learning who could relate these insights to the social and ethnic diversity of the student population. Where possible, some integration with a course dealing with the psychology and sociology of the community college would be desirable.

117

Community college teachers emphasized that offerings in language skills, if they are to have practical input, should be what they claim, giving teachers the opportunity to develop or improve specialized skills required by the particular context in which they find themselves. Resource persons should be involved as often as possible.

A similar caution was sounded in regard to area studies (contemporary culture, history, arts, literature, cinema, etc.). Unless the teaching staff understands clearly the nature of the endeavor and has the perspective necessary to develop what in our present framework represent "interdisciplinary" offerings, there is the risk of so-called "culture" courses being simply literary surveys in a new guise. Professors of a foreign language and literature who are more than passably knowledgeable in such areas as sociology, political science, and history would be encouraged to offer the kinds of courses which correspond to the current needs and interests of secondary school and community college FL teachers. Equally important, contributions should likewise be sought from professors of history, sociology and political science who have the necessary intimate knowledge of the language and culture in question.

A prerequisite to any of the above courses is first-hand experience in the culture of the particular language group. Study abroad should thus be a required component of all teacher preparation programs. Where this experience has not been included on the undergraduate level it should be gained prior to or as a part of any graduate-level work. In this connection, more effort needs to be made to examine and to recommend to community college FL teachers a variety of

camps, study programs, and work programs,
both abroad and in second-language communities within the United States.

8. PREPARING STAFF FOR THE JUNIOR-COMMUNITY COLLEGE

TERRY O'BANION
University of Illinois

With very few exceptions, preservice programs
for the preparation of junior-community college staff are grossly inadequate. The disciplines in the university are inflexible;
the colleges of education are unsure and un-
practiced. Available instructors are either
discipline-oriented, narrow, subject-matter
specialists or secondary-school-oriented,
college of education graduates. Neither is
prepared to instruct at the junior-community
college.

Junior-community college administrators
are outspoken in their criticism regarding
preservice programs:

Adapted from *The People Who Staff the
People's College*, A Report for the
National Advisory Council for Education
Development

120

There are practically no strong pre-
service collegiate programs for community staff members, and those that
are in operation provide only a small
fraction of the *qualified* personnel
needed. Increasing numbers of so-
called preservice programs have been
established, but they are too often
only "blisters" on School of Education
programs, and are generally inadequate
or worse than nothing. (Joseph Cosand,
Former President, St.Louis Junior College District, Missouri)

Preservice college and university programs are generally inadequate to our
needs, principally for lack of concern
with instructional purposes, learning,
and organization for instruction.
(Robert McCabe, Executive Vice President,
Miami-Dade Junior College, Florida)

In direct answer to the question, how
adequate are university preparation
programs, I would reply that with few
exceptions they missed the mark.
(Clyde Blocker, President, Harrisburg
Area Community College, Pennsylvania)

The situation is so intolerable that
some critics have suggested that universities
should not even attempt to prepare junior-
community college staff. These critics have
recommended that all available energies and
funds should be channeled into programs of
inservice education to be coordinated by the
colleges themselves.

It is academic, however, to argue
whether universities should prepare staff
for the junior-community college. The fact
is that universities do prepare staff and
will continue to do so. In the 1970's,

121

funds are needed to continue the outstanding
programs, to upgrade the inadequate programs,
and to develop new programs specifically designed for the preparation of junior-community college personnel.

DIMENSIONS OF PROGRAMS FOR JUNIOR-COMMUNITY
COLLEGE JUNIOR STAFF

Although the American Association of
Junior Colleges estimates that these are
approximately 100 graduate institutions
which offer programs that include the preparation of junior college faculty, there is
little evidence to suggest that these programs are adequate for the task. Too often
a single course is titled "The Junior College," and this course is the total experience of those who graduate from these "specialized" programs. The English instructor
takes the same sequence of literature courses
as the Ph.D. candidate--and a course in "The
Junior College." The counselor takes the
same sequence of counseling psychology--and
a course in "The Junior College." What is
more ludicrous, the course on "The Junior
College" is often taught by a professor who
has had no experience in and who has little
understanding of the community college.

The first qualities which a preservice
program must generate are an understanding of
the history and a commitment to the philosophy of the junior college. Staff members
must have knowledge of and appreciation for
characteristics common to this institution:
open-door, community service, teaching oriented student centeredness, comprehensive curriculum (career programs, developmental programs, general deucation, continuing education, and transfer programs), etc. While
these characteristics are also present in
some other American educational systems, they

122

have developed special meaning in the community college; they combine to make this institution unlike any other in the nation and the world.

The second recommendation is as important as the first. This recommendation is for preservice programs which facilitate staff understanding and acceptance of the students who attend the community college. The diversity of students in age, ability, socioeconomic background, ethnic background, and personality characteristics is greater than in any other institution of higher education. The prospective college staff member must be keenly aware of this diversity and he must be able to provide a wide range of learning experiences for these students. Above all, he must believe that these students can learn.

In addition to these two basic dimensions of a special program, an internship is strongly recommended for all staff members who would work in a junior college. For instructors, the internship should be under the supervision of a master teacher at the college level. For counselors and administrators, supervision should be provided by highly competent personnel in these fields. The internship should be a paid experience, and the intern should be a member of the staff-- to assist his full involvement in the institution. While the university should assist in coordinating the internship program, the primary responsibility should be given to the junior college. The commitment of the college to the internship program is essential if quality experiences are to be provided to interns. Excellent cooperative intern programs that could serve as models have been developed in several regions.

The length of internship should be sufficient for the prospective staff member's immersion in his potential area of expertise. Most internships should extend for at least a full term (semester, quarter, trimester). Special internships may extend for a full year. In some cases, mini-internships and rotating internships may be appropriate.

An understanding of the philosophy and history of the junior-community college, a knowledge and appreciation of the college students, and an internship are three dimensions which should be included in any program designed to prepare staff for such institutions. In addition, instructors must have an understanding of the learning process and be acquainted with new approaches and innovations in learning.

While community colleges have loudly claimed to be "teaching institutions," they might be sadly quiet if they ever examined their true production of student learning. Given the mission of the college and the challenge of the student, the quality of the teaching-learning process is woefully inadequate. Many instructors for these institutions do not know *how* to teach, and they are not helped to know *how* in most teacher education programs. Present approaches, professor modeling and methodology courses, are primitive and weak. Hopefully, the advances in micro-teaching, systems learning, encounter groups, and other learning technologies will provide improved bases for teacher education programs.

In addition to learning about the process of learning, instructors must be aware of new approaches and innovations in education. Behavioral objectives, multimedia systems, audio-tutorial systems, computer-assisted learn-

ing, micro-groups, and many other approaches
need to be studied so that instructors can
adapt these to their own styles.

So far, this section has sketched minimal requirements for the improvement of graduate preparation programs for community college staff. However, another requirement
the development of the "humanistic" personality, is more important than all the others,
for ultimately this personality distinguishes
the superior from the inferior educator.
The superior "humanistic" educator values
human beings. He believes that all human
beings can learn; he is deeply committed to
the facilitation of human development--on a
variety of levels in a variety of ways. His
style is to challenge, encourage, support,
stimulate, encounter. He is knowledgeable,
creative, imaginatitive, and innovative. He
is essential if the junior college is to come
to full fruition as the "people's college"
in the 70's.

A TEACHING DEGREE FOR THE JUNIOR-COMMUNITY
COLLEGE

Existing major degrees have not been
appropriate for those who would *teach* in a
junior-community college. The master's degree in a subject matter field often means
too narrow course specialization and no instruction in the junior college and teaching
methodology. Most subject matter degrees are
lock-step routes for potential doctoral students in a discipline. On the other hand
the master of education degree has been
criticized because it fails to offer sufficient preparation in the subject matter field.

The Ph.D degree emphasizes specialized
knowledge and research. Thus, it has been

125

one of the least appropriate degrees for the
community college instructor. The Ph.D. has
been the admission ticket into the professional ranks of the university; those whose
goal is the "community of scholars" in the
university experience "transfer shock" when
they come to the community college. The Ed.D.
degree, while appropriate for administrators
and counselors, suffers from the same limitation as the M.Ed.; it lacks sufficient depth
in subject matter to make it an appropriate
degree for instructors.

Degrees beyond the master's but less than
the doctorate -Advanced Certificate, Specialist in Education, and the self-awarded A.B.D.
- have been available for many years. They
are not, however, degrees that have been held
in high regard.

In recent years, new interest has developed in an advanced teaching degree that extends beyond the one-year master's and requires a different orientation than the re-
search-based Ph.D. It is possible to redesign the Ph.D.as a teaching degree, but
most effort has been in the direction of new
degrees. Some colleges and universities
have developed the two-year Master of Arts in
College Teaching. Others have experimented
with the Doctorate of Arts in Teaching. The
Carnegie Corporation has provided considerable support for the development of D.A. programs in a number of universities. The D.A.
degree is more likely to emerge as the favor-
ed degree of those who would teach in a junior college.

An advanced teaching degree appears to
be ideally designed for the highly competent
instructors required in the junior-community
college. It is imperative, of course, that
such degrees include the core of special ex-

126

periences outlined in the preceding section. In addition, careful consideration should be given to the nature of the subject matter content in these new degrees.

There is unanimous agreement that instructors coming to the community college must be highly competent in their subject matter field. No one suggests that instructors should not be well grounded in content. But too few question the validity of the kind of content in which these instructors are highly competent. An English instructor with thirty to forty hours of specialized graduate literature courses is not necessarily prepared to teach three sections of composition and one section of American literature in the junior college. How does a specialization in medieval history help an instructor teach western civilization or American institutions or social problems? How does an advanced degree in experimental psychology help an instructor teach courses in personal development? Is the content of a degree in art history sufficient for the instructor of a course in humanities? Can a physics major bring the appropriate teaching competences to a course in general science?

The problem extends beyond the failure of universities to supplement "content" courses with classes in the junior-community college and learning theory; most often, the "content" courses themselves are inappropriate for the needs of college faculty. Graduate students and junior college instructors need to question the traditional content of degree programs for the disciplines. They must work with willing colleges and universities to design more flexible and appropriate content programs for community college instructors. Hopefully, the advanced teach-

ing degree will be more than Ph.D. courses
minus the dissertation; better, a new degree
with different content and with a different
purpose. Universities are not going to aban-
don the Ph.D., but with a considerable financial support, many universities could develop
a teaching Ph.D. or D.A. degree that could
become a model preservice program for junior
college instructors.

ROLE OF THE JUNIOR-COMMUNITY COLLEGE

To insure the quality and implementation
of programs, universities must work closely
with area junior-community colleges.

Such colleges are usually quite willing
to provide practical and internship experiences for graduate students if these experiences are part of a well-designed university
program and coordinated by knowledgeable and
committed university personnel. Some community colleges have even provided pay and staff
supervision for graduate interns.

In addition to graduate internships, the
colleges can provide experienced staff members as resources for university classes.
Projects and research studies can be carried
out by graduate students in the college.
Field trips, demonstrations, workshops, and
interviews can all be provided by the college.
College facilities, laboratories, and materials are often more sophisticated than those
available in the university.

The university must also develop cooperative relationships with business and industry,
possibly through the junior-community college,
for appropriate graduate programs. For those
universities that have the programs and staff
to prepare vocational and technical instructors, administrators, and counselors for the

college, cooperation with business and industry is most important.

The community college has another very important role in preservice programs. At many of these colleges, prospective instructors and paraprofessionals are currently students enrolled in the college. Therefore, programs which begin teacher education in these colleges need to be carefully coordinated with university programs to avoid duplication of efforts and to insure ease of student transfer. Universities and junior colleges should develop flexible but consistent career ladders to assist students as they explore the roles of paraprofessionals, instructors, or administrators.

COOPERATING UNIVERSITIES

If universities are to be chiefly responsible for the creation of quality preparation programs for junior-community college staff, then the universities must be qualified to do it. The following guidelines propose minimal qualifications for universities:

1) *The university staff must be knowledgeable and experienced regarding the junior-community college.*
One of the great complaints regarding present university programs in that the professors coordinating these programs have no experience in the community college. Scruggs (1969) surveyed 102 four-year colleges and universities that offered one or more courses in the junior college. Of 131 professors teaching these courses, only 7 had community college experience; 81 had never been inside a junior college.

If universities wish to develop these programs, they should recruit qualified pro-

129

fessionals from the colleges themselves.
This is no easy task because practitioners
in the junior college often do not have the
publishing and research backgrounds required
for major positions in the universities.
Too, universities can seldom offer salaries
to match those earned by staff who hold leadership positions in community colleges.
Special funds must be available to the university so that these college leaders can be
attracted to develop staff preservice programs. If highly respected and knowledgeable
junior college professionals cannot be attracted to the university, then these programs will encounter great difficulty in
meeting the needs of the college.

2) *The university must be willing to develop
cooperative relationships with junior-community colleges.*
    While universities have primary responsi-
bility for program development, junior-community colleges have an important role to play
in the preservice education of staff for
these institutions. Key personnel from community colleges should be involved in all
levels of university program planning. An
advisory committee from these colleges should
meet periodically with university staff to
plan program objectives, determine curriculum,
recruit staff and students, arrange facilities, provide internships, organize research,
develop inservice programs which complement
the preservice program, and develop evaluation schema for the preservice program.

    Junior-community colleges should have
primary responsibility for coordinating and
supervising the university student internships. Funds should be available for supervision and for the interns' salaries to insure that the internship is a quality experience. The university should appoint key per-

130

sonnel in the college as adjunct university
staff to encourage cooperation. Staff in
many of the colleges have attained a high
level of professionalization in the last decade and can be expected to perform supervisory roles as well as if not better than university staff.

3) *The university should be adjacent to a
number of outstanding junior-community colleges so that cooperative programs can be
developed.*
     If there is to be constant interaction
between the university and the junior college, then it is more likely to occur when
well developed colleges are in close proximity to the university. Some of the best
universities in the country have three or
four junior colleges within commuting distance; some, especially in urban centers,
have many more.

     It is possible, of course, to provide
internships in community colleges which are
not adjacent to the university, but close
proximity is an advantage for the internship
and for the many other cooperative relationships that should be developed.

4) *The university should be an outstanding
university in American education, or it
should have some special attributes for developing a program for junior-community college staff, or both.*
     If a new degree for a new kind of person
in a new kind of institution is to have any
success, then it must have support from the
eminent universities in this country. The
venture into the D.A. cannot be left to the
state colleges-lately-become-universities.
Only the major universities have, for the
most part, the expertise in subject matter
and in educational methodology which are

131

needed in these new staff development programs.

In the present decade, the great glut of Ph.D.'s will force universities to reexamine their compulsive commitment to a one-dimensional model of excellence. With available funds these universities can be encouraged to develop the imaginative and nontraditional preservice programs required for community college staff.

There are some institutions of higher education that should be encouraged to develop programs because of their special qualifications to do so. Examples include the Union Graduate School, the upper-level universities, and the California state colleges.

The Union Graduate School, based at Antioch College is a bold experiment in graduate education that offers a great deal of promise for those who wish to be prepared for the junior college. The School's program is creative and flexible. It provides a structure of education for graduate students which is similar to the structure in which they will teach. The program experiences are often based in community colleges.

Upper-level universities have been designed to complement junior colleges. Florida Atlantic University, the University of West Florida, Sangamon State University and Governor's State University in Illinois, the new systems in Texas and Alaska are examples and others are being developed. These universities are potential homes for significant junior college staff development programs. They are dependent on the colleges, since they enroll no freshman or sophomore students. They have developed excellent systems of cooperation with area colleges. Their staffs

132

often include personnel who are knowledgeable and experienced in the college. These universities have not had time to become encrusted with traditional graduate approaches to education. Finally, the great majority of their students have attended community colleges and thus have at least some familiarity with the institution for which their graduate program would be designed.

The California state colleges have a history of commitment to and involvement with the junior college movement. They have developed teacher education and student personnel programs that need to be continued and developed further.

A number of eminent and special colleges and universities meet the requirements outlined in this section. Many of them have been providing excellent staff preparation programs for a number of years. These programs should be expanded. However, if real impact is to be made, a great many more programs will need to be developed in this decade.

9. JUNIOR-SENIOR COLLEGE ARTICULATION PROBLEMS

ERNEST F. ANDERSON
University of Illinois

One definition of articulation is "the action or manner of jointing or interrelating." The jointing or interrelating of junior-community colleges and senior colleges and universities probably began in 1901 with the establishment of the first public junior college at Joliet, Illinois, as a part of the Joliet Township High School. This process of the articulation of academic programs between two- and four-year institutions has grown with the increase in the number of two-year colleges and the number and proportion of students enrolled in those institutions who desire to transfer into baccalaureate-oriented programs at four-year colleges and universities. The function of articulation between junior and senior colleges has become a speciality, and in Illinois, approximately 20 institutions have assigned individuals as coordinators of University-Junior College Relations. Junior colleges are also

134

assigning personnel as coordinators of Senior College Relations.

   The need for professional assistance in the process of articulation to the junior and senior colleges is demonstrated by the number of transfer students who begin their academic careers at one institution and decide for whatever reason to move (transfer) from one institution to another during an academic year. For example, during the 1967-68 academic year, approximately 30,000 students transferred within the state of Illinois.[1] Of this number, more than 18,000 transferred during the fall term. Further data on transfers emphasizes the need for articulation.

1) Private institutions send more transfers than they receive.
2) Public senior colleges receive more transfers than they send.
3) Public junior colleges receive more transfers than they send.
4) There are more transfers from senior colleges to junior colleges than from junior colleges to senior colleges.
5) More than one-third of the transfers to four-year colleges and universities are concentrated in the curricula of teacher education, and 25 percent are in the area of liberal arts with approximately 14 percent in commerce and business administration.

Clearly potential articulation problems are great in a state as large as Illinois with 30,000 or more students transferring each year.

   One of the interesting articulation problems in Illinois institutions of higher education is that there are as many transfers

among four-year colleges and universities as
there are between two- and four-year institutions. At the University of Illinois over
the last four-year period (1968-71) more than
half of the total new transfer students have
been transfers from another four-year college
or university. In 1971, approximately 60
percent of all transfers to the University of
Illinois at Urbana-Champaign last attended
another four-year college or university.
However, the University of Illinois at
Chicago Circle receives about three times
as many transfers in the fall as the University of Illinois at Urbana-Champaign, and
about two-thirds of the transfers at that
urban university are from four-year colleges.
The data show clearly that there are fewer
junior college transfers at the University
of Illinois than transfers from other types
of institution. However, at Southern
Illinois University and Eastern Illinois
University this is not the case. Therefore,
articulation problems are not just problems
between two- and four-year institutions, but
there are problems of interrelationships
between two- and four-year institutions,
among four-year colleges and universities
and among two-year junior and community
colleges.

STATEWIDE ARTICULATION PROBLEMS

1) *Numbers*. There are 37 public junior
college districts and 46 campuses enrolling
70,000 full-time and part-time students in
baccalaureate oriented curricula. These students are planning to enter more than 50 Illinois and numerous out-of-state colleges and
universities to study for the bachelor's degree. Possibilities for conflict in inte-
grating the programs completed by these students into the baccalaureate programs at the
institutions to which these students trans-

fer makes it mandatory that these problems
be solved and transfer made more routine if
we are to develop an integrated system of
higher education.

2) *General education requirements.* Junior colleges which develop their own general
education requirements for the associate degree find that their graduates may not have
met the lower division general education requirements at the senior institutions when
they transfer. The general education requirements are usually different among institutions, and at major universities they vary
among the different colleges on a single
campus. In some cases, the courses required
vary according to the curriculum entered.
This means that a junior college student or
a student at another four-year institution
planning to transfer to the University of
Illinois and major in a specific area must
usually select his general education requirements in relation to the curriculum that he
will enter. Knowledgeable junior college
personnel know that most junior college
freshmen have not made a firm decision about
the college to which they plan to transfer
and certainly have not decided on the specific curriculum they expect to enter.

3) *Major requirements.* The major requirements are different at the various senior
colleges and universities for the same major
and are not clearly communicated to the junior college students and counselors at many
institutions. Courses which will count towards a degree at one institution may not
count towards the same degree in the same way
at another institution. This makes it almost
necessary that a student select his courses
during his freshman and sophmore years at a
junior college or other university to meet
the requirements of the institution from

which the student expects to receive his degree if he expects to graduate without loss of credit.

4) *Career programs.* Junior colleges are comprehensive institutions and many of them offer vocational-technical or career program courses which are usually not applicable to most bachelor's degrees at a university. Students do not always understand why they cannot graduate in two years after transfer if they have completed an associate's degree at a junior college and are accepted for transfer at a four-year institution. They fail to understand-or at least to accept-the specialized content requirements expected for the various four-year programs.

5) *Course definition.* Some of the courses offered by junior-community colleges are considered by four-year colleges and universities as upper division (junior and senior) courses and, therefore, not applicable to be counted towards the bachelor's degree. At other institutions the same course may be labeled as lower division.

6) *Space-limitation for transfers in the specialized curricula.* Some comprehensive institutions offer curricula which are only available at one institution in the state and, in many cases, those institutions are unable to admit all qualified applicants. This usually happens in the professional curricula such as veterinary science, pre-medicine, architecture, and art. In many cases, transfer students do not understand that even though they may have an outstanding academic record, they cannot be accepted because of limitations of space and facilities.

These six articulation problems are all prevalent in Illinois and can probably be identified in any state.

FOREIGN LANGUAGE ARTICULATION PROBLEMS

Only a very few of the total junior college enrollment expect to enter curricula which require a FL. A much smaller percentage expect to major in a FL. Those who do find that junior colleges do not offer courses other than the beginning two years of a foreign language and, in many cases, offer only one language. The characteristics of junior college students in general, combined with their vocational orientation and lack of concentration in the humanities and arts, make it unlikely that junior colleges will employ large components of faculty and develop programs for FL majors. This means that it is unlikely that there will be enough students to support a fully developed FL program in more than one or two languages in junior colleges with less than 2,000 students.

A second problem is that the few students who do complete four years of language in high school find that they must wait for two years while enrolled in a junior college before they are able to take more advanced foreign language courses. This is because most junior colleges are not authorized to offer the more advanced foreign language courses which are considered in some states to be upper division courses.

A third problem of articulation in foreign language courses found in the alternative provided for the major proportion of students who never plan to transfer. The study of FL as a general education requirement for all junior college students is discussed by many and approved by few. However, the logic of the situation is such that it may be more important for junior college students to study and understand foreign culture than for the smaller number of university graduates to have profited from this experience. Yet, if language is developed as a general education requirement in junior colleges and if it is different in content from the present lower division FL courses, how will the universities evaluate it when students change their mind and ask that it be accepted for transfer?

Approximately 38 percent of the transfer students to the University of Illinois in the Fall of 1970 had completed the FL requirement of four years of high school work or sixteen semester hours. Only 26 percent of the junior college transfers had completed the FL requirement while 45 percent of the four-year college transfers and 42 percent of a sample of native students had completed it. Approximately one-half of the females from all three groups of transfer students had completed the language requirement while 19 percent of the junior college males and approximately one-third of the four-year transfers and natives had completed the same requirement.

BACKGROUND OF I.B.H.E. ARTICULATION
RECOMMENDATION

The Illinois Board of Higher Education appointed a nineteen-member articulation study committee in 1970 representing public and non-public, two- and four-year colleges, and elementary and secondary schools. The Advisory Committee made the following two recommendations which were approved in June 1971 by the Illinois Board of Higher Education and sent to the Presidents of all

Illinois colleges and universities for consideration.

1) *Illinois public junior college transfer students in good standing who have completed an associate degree in a baccalaureate-oriented curriculum should be considered as having met the lower division general education requirements of the senior institution.* A study of the records of a random sample of Fall 1971 junior college transfers at Urbana-Champaign shows that 39 percent had completed an associate's degree and 14 percent of the 1970 junior college transfers at Chicago had completed an associate's degree.

2) *Junior and senior colleges should cooperate in developing "mutually-agreed-upon" transfer programs.* Such programs should (a) be in writing; (b) include satisfaction of the senior institution's lower division general education requirements for associate degree holders continuing in the same field; and (c) provide for acceptance toward the degree of all other transfer courses in the mutually agreed upon programs for students continuing in the same field.

I will be meeting soon with appropriate Deans at Urbana-Champaign and Chicago Circle to explore with them what progress we can report to the Illinois Board of Higher Education in regard to the implementation of the recommendations.

I will also be meeting with junior college representatives along with campus coordinators and college representatives to explore the possibility of using the *Transfer*

141

*Handbook for Junior College Students,
Academic Advisors and Counselors*[2] which
contains "suggested two-year programs" as a
basis for developing mutually agreed upon
curricula with junior colleges.

SUMMARY

It is my belief that the institutions,
colleges, or departments that are prepared
to accept the A. A. degree as meeting lower
division general education requirements and
are also willing to mutually agree with
junior colleges on the content to be included
in the first two years of a transfer program
are more likely to attract an increasing
number of junior college transfers than
institutions or units which do not make such
a change in educational requirements.
Through this process of program articulation
we can solve many of the problems for these
junior college transfer students who complete an associate's degree.

NOTES

1. Anderson, Ernest F., G. Robert Darnes,
   Irma T. Halfter and Henry Moughamian,
   *Performance of Transfer Students Within
   Illinois Institutions of Higher Educa-
   tion*, 544 Iles Park Place, Springfield,
   Illinois, 1971, 52 pp.

2. Harshbarger, James T. and Jack K. Salmon
   (ed): *A Transfer Handbook for Junior
   College Students, Academic Advisors,
   and Counselors*, School-College Relations,
   Office of Admissions and Records, University of Illinois, Urbana, Illinois, 1971.

SECTION III:

FACTS

AND

FIGURES

10. FOREIGN LANGUAGES IN TWO-YEAR COLLEGES— ALIVE AND WELL, OR SICK AND TIRED?

GERALD F. HICKEY
Hutchinson Community Junior College
Hutchinson, Kansas

In the fall of 1971, I designed a questionnaire to be sent to the foreign language departments of two-year colleges, seeking to establish the current status of FL study in them and the departments' estimates of strengths and problems.

The questionnaire went to some 200 colleges, and 71 institutions responded. Responding colleges are located in 17 states,

---

Paper presented at session on "What is Happening to Students in Junior College Foreign Languages" at Central States Conference on the Teaching of Foreign Languages, Chicago, 1972.

145

principally west of the Mississippi; the largest numbers of replies came from Kansas (12) and Texas (10). Respondents included private liberal arts schools, public comprehensive community colleges, and technical institutions.

There were at least 9 different languages offered by the 71 colleges, but Spanish, French, and German accounted for nearly 90% of the 1971-72 enrollments and Spanish alone for nearly half. Percentages of the student body studying languages ranged from less than 1% to 33%; the median enrollment figure was 7.75% of the student population. Half the replies indicated that enrollments were rising or stable, half that numbers of students were on the decline. At least some students in half the colleges replying tend to take more than one year of foreign language study.

Seeking to assess reasons why students take languages, the departments listed motives ranging from job preparation and senior institution requirements to desire to travel for personal reasons or to do missionary work. Some said that their college was located in an area where a particular FL was spoken, others that students were interested in or curious about other tongues and other cultures. Still other commented that students expected to major or minor in languages, that student rapport with the foreign language faculty was good, and that counselors or advisers encouraged foreign language study.

In colleges where foreign language enrollment was rising or stable, departments noted overall growth of the college, heightened awareness and appreciation of other countries, cultures, and languages, shifts in transfer plans, and a number of significant internal changes: appointment of full-time (rather than part-time) faculty, utilization of native speakers as informants and teaching assistants, establishment of open classrooms with programmed instruction, introduction of contract grading systems (no D's or F's) and/or of variable credit options, encouragement of foreign language clubs or student councils, and the development of non-credit or mini-courses.

In colleges where foreign language enrollment was declining, departments tended to cite factors beyond their control: students' preoccupation with the "here and now," isolationist feelings in the community, reductions in foreign language requirements at transfer institutions, students' poor experiences with languages in high school, lack of cooperation from administrators, counselors and other faculty members, absence of or resistance to electives in vocational-technical curricula, overall decline in enrollment, unfavorable class schedules, and even the new draft policy. A question on attrition after initial enrollment in languages elicited similar answers with the further comments that students found the basic FL courses difficult and time-consuming, irrelevant and impractical, or had no aptitude or time for language study.

A question on innovative approaches and techniques in use or under consideration produced reports of college sponsored song-fests, clubs, dinners, and tours (chiefly to Mexico), cooperative tutoring programs with FLES and high school classes and with native speakers and advanced students, development

of "packets" (units, modules) and other
individualized materials, and many ingenious
uses of audio-visual and resource-center
materials and devices.

   Discussion of the results of this survey
at the Central States Conference produced
several suggestions: 1) that foreign language teachers take the initiative in contacting counselors and administrators and
providing them with up-to-date materials on
the value of language study, particularly
for non-transfer students; 2) that teachers
tap all possible resources in the community
(bilinguals, native speakers, persons with
travel experience) and bring them to their
students; 3) that teachers explore pass-fail
options, contract grading, variable credit
systems, and extended "incomplete" grades,
to lessen the pressures on students' time;
4) that teachers constantly seek new kinds
of courses that would be serviceable to the
community (refresher, literacy, and conversation courses, the development of specialized vocabulary and structure, etc.); and
5) that teachers familiarize themselves with
recent developments in learning theory and
teaching strategies and apply these in their
classrooms.

CONCLUSION

   My findings indicate that foreign language study in two-year colleges, while not
without problem areas, is in a relatively
encouraging state. Enrollments in the 71
reporting colleges had increased by nearly
1/3 from 1970 to 1971, and in the three most
popular languages (Spanish, French and
German) and in Latin by 60%. But the reasons
for this growth frequently included either

newness of the institution or newness of the
program or of some aspect of it (a new language offered, new courses, etc.) In established institutions, increase in FL enrollment does not seem to be keeping pace with
overall growth. This is a trend which should
be watched. Growth patterns did not seem to
be significantly different in public, private
or church related institutions. Administra-
tions seemed to be taking a generally favorable view of FL courses and teachers, and
energetic, enthusiastic instructors were
capitalizing on the opportunities available
to them. Increases and reductions in FL
faculty time appeared about to balance out.
Student resistance was sometimes augmented
by counselors' or other students' advice,
but in some institutions it seemed to be
lessening. Attrition after the basic courses
was a widespread phenomenon, but steps were
being taken to deal with it at a number of
colleges. In short, the patient, Mr. FL in
two-year colleges, cannot report glowing
health at this time, but he certainly isn't
dead yet!

A. STATES REPRESENTED IN QUESTIONNAIRE AND
   NUMBER OF REPLIES FROM EACH STATE:

    Arizona 2
    Arkansas. 3
    Colorado. 4
    Florida 1
    Idaho 1
    Indiana 3
    Iowa 8
    Kansas. 12
    Louisiana 1
    Minnesota 6

```
Missouri. . . . . . . . 8
Nebraska. . . . . . . . 3
North Dakota. . . . . . 1
Oklahoma. . . . . . . . 2
South Dakota. . . . . . 1
Texas . . . . . . . . .10
Wyoming . . . . . . . . 4
Not Identified. . . . . 1
                        ─

Total Reporting
Institutions  . . . . .71
(200 questionnaires sent out)
```

B. 1970-1971 ENROLLMENT - GRAND TOTALS BY
   LANGUAGES (71 INSTITUTIONS):

```
Dutch . . . . . . . . . 0
French. . . . . . . . .1693
German. . . . . . . . .1405
Greek . . . . . . . . 159
Hebrew. . . . . . . .  19
Italian . . . . . . .   8
Latin . . . . . . . .  32
Russian . . . . . . .  55
Spanish . . . . . . .2919
Independent Study . .   0
Others (Languages
   Not Identified) . .3223
                       ────

                      9513
```

C. 1970-71 ENROLLMENTS IN ORDER OF
   IMPORTANCE (71 INSTITUTIONS):

```
Spanish . . . . . . .2919
French. . . . . . . .1693
German. . . . . . . .1405
Greek . . . . . . . . 159
Russian . . . . . . .  55
Latin . . . . . . . .  32
Hebrew. . . . . . . .  19
```

```
Italian . . . . . . .    8
Dutch . . . . . . . .    0
Independent Study . .    0
                      ──────
                       6290
```

D. 1971-1972 ENROLLMENT - GRAND TOTALS BY
   LANGUAGES (71 INSTITUTIONS):

```
Dutch . . . . . . . .    9
French. . . . . . . .2368
German. . . . . . . .1609
Greek . . . . . . .  95
Hebrew. . . . . . .  19
Italian . . . . . .  14
Latin . . . . . . .  92
Russian . . . . . .  19
Spanish . . . . . .4238
Independent Study . .  1
Others (Languages
   Not Identified) . . 816
                      ──────
                       9280
```

E. 1971-1972 ENROLLMENTS IN ORDER OF
   IMPORTANCE (71 INSTITUTIONS):

```
Spanish . . . . . . .4238
French. . . . . . . .2368
German. . . . . . . .1609
Greek . . . . . . .  95
Latin . . . . . . .  92
Hebrew. . . . . . .  19
Russian . . . . . .  19
Italian . . . . . .  14
Dutch . . . . . . .   9
Independent Study . .  1
                      ──────
                       8464
```

Difference between 1971-72 and 1970-71
Grand Totals: 233 students

F. WHAT PERCENTAGE OF THE STUDENT BODY
   ENROLLS IN FOREIGN LANGUAGE?
   (71 REPORTING INSTITUTIONS)

   1 school   .017%
   3 schools   1%
   4 schools   2%
   1 school   2.5%
   4 schools   3%
   1 school   3.7%
   6 schools   4%
   1 school   4.5%
   7 schools   5%
   2 schools   5.5%
   1 school   5.6%
   1 school   6%
   1 school   7%
   1 school   7.5%
   1 school   7.75%
   2 schools   8%
   1 school   8.4%
   4 schools   9%
   7 schools   10%
   1 school   11%
   1 school   11.08%
   4 schools   12%
   1 school   13%
   1 school   14%
   1 school   16%
   1 school   20%
   1 school   25%
   1 school   30%
   1 school   33%
   9 schools did not report a percentage
                                    figure.
G. WHAT ARE THE MAIN REASONS GIVEN BY
   STUDENTS FOR ENROLLING IN FOREIGN
   LANGUAGES?

   1) Interest in foreign languages.
   2) To complete curriculum requirements

152

for certain occupations.
3) To fulfill senior institution requirements.
4) For credit.
5) They appreciate the aesthetic and
cultural value of a foreign language.
6) They are language minors or majors.
7) Personal reason (not identified in
questionnaire).
8) Good student-teacher rapport.
9) To enter ministry or to do missionary
work.
10) Students want to "try" a foreign language.
11) Counselors and faculty advisors encouraged them to enroll in foreign
language(s).
12) Students want to broaden general
education background.
13) The college is located in an area
where foreign language(s) is spoken.
14) Students want to brush up on a prior
language knowledge.
15) Bilinguals want to learn written language.
16) Travel.

H. DO BEGINNING STUDENTS TEND TO TAKE MORE
THAN THE BASIC TWO SEMESTERS OF A FOREIGN
LANGUAGE?

Yes . . . . 17 out of 71 reporting
institutions.
No. . . . . 28 out of 71 reporting
institutions.
Some. . . . 20 out of 71 reporting
institutions.
No answer . 6 out of 71 reporting
institutions.

I. IF STUDENTS DO NOT ADVANCE BEYOND BASIC
   COURSES, WHY DO THEY QUIT LANGUAGES AT
   THIS POINT?

1) Students switch to courses which will
   prepare them for employment.
2) Students have completed curriculum or
   graduation requirements.
3) Few students can afford to travel to
   countries where they could apply what
   they have learned.
4) Lack of ability.
5) They have satisfied transfer institution requirements.
6) College does not have offerings beyond
   basic courses.
7) Credit is easier to obtain in other
   courses.
8) Language courses compete with courses
   that students deem more essential.
9) There is a lack of interest in major-
   ing in a foreign language.
10) Students wish to spend more time in
    their own field of interest.
11) Counselors advise students not to go
    on with language study.
12) Foreign languages are too difficult
    and too time consuming.
13) Too many students enroll in foreign
    languages as sophomores and leave the
    program at the end of one year.
14) High school students enter college but
    do not have the desire to continue
    foreign language study.
15) Students do not see why they should
    study foreign languages.
16) Schedule conflicts limit enrollment in
    foreign languages.
17) The basic courses seem irrelevant and
    impractical.

18) Other courses require so much work that students do not have the time to study foreign languages.
19) Students do not want a course which demands disciplined, consistent study.
20) Foreign language program is too new to have advanced courses.
21) Students prefer courses where easy *A, B, C* can be obtained.
22) Students have no aptitude for foreign languages.
23) Students lose interest.
24) Foreign language course won't fit into a tight schedule.
25) Most students need only so many hours of credit and thus will choose only courses required for a particular curriculum.
26) Students hear reports that foreign languages are difficult so they will choose other options.
27) Grading system places too much pressure on academic average, grading system should be *Pass* or *No Credit*.
28) There is a lack of realistic career goals within language field.
29) There is no point in taking a foreign language if it is not directly applicable in a student's job.
30) Basic courses fulfill humanities requirement.
31) Mid-term transfer to senior institutions.
32) There is no space for foreign language in technical and scientific programs.
33) Students transfer to a teacher training program or to a terminal program, neither of which requires foreign language.
34) Area high school students take languages in high school and then enroll

155

in universities, not in local junior colleges.
35) Students plan to pick up languages later.
36) Students want to transfer to a college which does not have a foreign language requirement.
37) Only basic language courses are offered.
38) Students do not plan foreign travel, graduate work, or other projects that make a foreign language desirable.
39) Students change to majors that do not require foreign languages.
40) Basic courses frustrate students.
41) Unrealistic expectations, content and methods are not in keeping with student's goals.
42) Poor background in English hinders understanding of the grammar of the foreign language.
43) There is a lack of an exclusively conversational approach.

J. HAS FOREIGN LANGUAGE ENROLLMENT BEEN DECLINING OR INCREASING DURING THE PAST SEVERAL YEARS?

Increasing. . 23 out of 71 reporting institutions.
Decreasing. . 34 out of 71 reporting institutions.
Neither . . . 13 out of 71 reporting institutions.
Fluctuating . 1 out of 71 reporting institutions.

K. ARE THERE ANY REASONS FOR A DECLINE IN
   FOREIGN LANGUAGE ENROLLMENT IN YOUR
   COURSES?

1) Decrease in school enrollment.
2) Students feel no need to take a foreign
   language.
3) Senior institutions have dropped
   foreign language requirement.
4) Interest in humanities has been
   decreasing.
5) Foreign language is considered too
   difficult by students.
6) It takes a long time for a department
   to establish a reputation.
7) School requirements have been lowered.
8) School is deemphasizing foreign languages.
9) The nation's deemphasis of international affairs as seen by the generally
   career-oriented community college student.
10) It takes too much time to study a
    foreign language.
11) The students are living for the moment
    and are less concerned about degrees
    and requirements.
12) There has been a lack of efficient
    counseling.
13) Students do not see the relevancy of a
    foreign language.
14) Former students have had negative
    experiences with foreign languages and
    tend to influence other students.
15) Counselors are ill-prepared to over-
    come negative influences.
16) No interest in foreign languages is
    expressed by school administration.
17) With expanding curricula students have
    more options and tend to choose other
    areas of study.

18) Counselors do not "sell" languages.
19) Students are not aware of job possibilities in foreign languages.
20) There is a general lack of interest in foreign languages.
21) A raise in tuition is causing more selectivity in elective choices.
22) Students are more interested in vocationally oriented courses.
23) Foreign language classes are scheduled at unpopular times (afternoon).
24) Language enrollment was declining at such a rate that school decided not to fight declining trend.
25) There is an attitude of general isolation.
26) Students are from small communities where foreign languages are not emphasized and are thus ill-prepared to take college language courses and are afraid of languages.
27) Students have had unfortunate experiences with high school language courses.
28) Society is so technologically minded that students do not wish to take anything that has no immediate application in their major courses.
29) There is a failure to realize the advantage of a foreign language in the lives of the students.
30) Majority of students are student nurses and are not required to take a foreign language.
31) The opening of schools of technology and biomedical arts and sciences has cut enrollment in arts and sciences where the language students are.
32) French decreased to cancellation point. School is trying again with German and Spanish.

33) New draft policy.
34) Other electives are easier than foreign languages.
35) It is fashionable to omit language study.
36) Some high school teachers tell their students not to enroll in college language courses but to take tests for college credit for high school courses because students "have always studied everything the college offers," thus equating high school study with college study.
37) College counselors do not encourage advisees to take foreign languages and tend to underrate language study because some universities have dropped language requirements.
38) Emphasis on vocational approach to college tends to direct students away from any of the humanities courses.

L. ARE THERE ANY REASONS FOR AN INCREASE IN FOREIGN LANGUAGE ENROLLMENT IN YOUR COLLEGE?

1) Increased awareness of the value of foreign languages.
2) Interest in other countries and their cultures.
3) College is growing in enrollment.
4) Faculty advisors guide advisees into foreign languages.
5) More students are transferring to senior institutions.
6) A decreasing number of students is entering teacher training where foreign language is not a requirement.
7) A new foreign language curriculum has been established and efforts are being made to attract students to it.

8) New teachers are replacing older teachers.
9) A new junior college is building a foreign language program.
10) There has been an increase in enrollment, but a peaking point is being reached.
11) Foreign language is required in certain curricula.
12) Curriculum has been changed from strictly night-time study to day and night study by hiring a full-time teacher.
13) As college enrollment rises, community college gets more language students.
14) Continuity has been established by the hiring of a permanent full-time teacher (language can be offered every semester instead of intermittently).
15) College has established multi-level "open classrooms" for elementary and intermediate courses, using programmed instruction to make this possible.
16) Department is governed by a student delegate council.
17) Department has promised that no D's or F's will be given, that students will be given opportunity to keep working beyond the end of the semester if need be to earn grades they feel will be acceptable.
18) Variable credit is given. Students can enroll for any number of credits (1-5) per semester in elementary or intermediate French.
19) College has established a course in conversational French.
20) College has established one credit mini-courses in French Pronunciation and France Today.

21) Enrollment is increasing but percentage of total school enrollment keeps dropping.
22) Foreign language program (only 3 years old) is popular.
23) A particular junior college has had a temporary increase because of a Dutch missionary who is training young people in Dutch so they will be able to do missionary work in Holland.
24) A new junior college is growing in enrollment.
25) Interest of students who come from small communities where they have had no previous opportunity to study foreign languages.
26) Foreign language curriculum has added second year courses.
27) College has an active foreign language club.
28) Addition of another language which has increased total language enrollment.
29) Students are interested in traveling to other countries.
30) Students are interested in foreign languages.
31) Foreign languages are elective courses.
32) Department is contacting area high schools to make them aware of college language programs.

M. WHAT INNOVATIVE METHODS OF TEACHING AND OTHER DEVICES ARE BEING USED TO CREATE MORE INTEREST IN FOREIGN LANGUAGE?

1) The foreign language department conducts trips to Mexico four times a year.
2) The faculty uses films and slides (some of their own manufacture).

161

3) Teacher introduces material of a
   nature to generate discussion in the
   target language.
4) Use of a language laboratory.
5) Department has a tutorial program.
6) Department has conversation as well as
   grammar courses.
7) Department utilizes records and tapes.
8) Students discuss pictures furnished by
   teacher.
9) Students discuss everyday foreign life.
10) The department uses professional
    lecturers.
11) The best Spanish students help teacher
    in a Saturday morning program for
    elementary children.
12) Opera librettos are reproduced so stu-
    dents can follow arias.
13) Drawing from foreign language maga-
    zines, the class has accumulated a
    collection of slides of advertisements
    which offer American products from a
    French or Spanish viewpoint.
14) The department uses audio-lingual
    methods of teaching.
15) The department uses many audio-visual
    materials.
16) Emphasis is on the practical aspects
    of learning foreign languages.
17) The department has individualized
    materials.
18) The department is adding audio equip-
    ment.
19) The department is shifting to "cultural
    pluralism" as principal goal.
20) Every Friday all classes are divided
    into small conversational groups.
21) The department sponsors yearly trip to
    Mexico.
22) Students describe each other.

23) Maps are utilized to identify cultural areas.
24) Once a week students give a report about some Spanish speaking country.
25) For one semester a Chilean student came almost every Tuesday, taught pronunciation, and also worked with individuals during the last half of the class period.
26) The teacher presents humorous magazine pictures and asks students to write stories about them.
27) Students translate articles from newspapers and magazines.
28) Students listen to tapes 3-5 times and then fill in items on an outline (in a booklet written in both Spanish and English).
29) The department uses a combination of aural-oral and traditional methods.
30) Teachers make use of foreign visitors or travelers.
31) The teacher encourages class to bring subject matter material to classroom.
32) The teacher stresses communication, not grammar.
33) The department is studying behavioral objectives as applied to foreign languages.
34) The college is moving toward development of "packets" of instruction (somewhat self-instructional) with very closely defined behavioral objectives and performance rates. One pilot program will probably be run in foreign languages. Unless there are policy or administrative changes, eventually all foreign languages will convert to "packet" instruction.
35) Students study and utilize materials specifically prepared for individ-

ualized instruction.
36) A church school brings in church personnel who have worked in countries where target language is spoken.
37) Efforts are made to use language in classroom.
38) The department conducts a study tour of Mexico during interterm.
39) The college conducts a summer session with 3-4 weeks spent in Mexico (session aimed at high school juniors and seniors).
40) The teacher conducts round table discussions in target language; new vocabulary and grammatical structures are used.
41) Students act out situations suggested by teacher.
42) The college joins with another junior college in a Christmas tour to Mexico.
43) The department uses leniency in course requirements and in grading students.
44) Students sing in target language.
45) Students take trips to local restaurants operated by Spanish-speaking people.
46) Students take a Spring trip to Monterrey, Mexico.
47) The department has a special review course for those entering third semester in a given language.
48) Once a week lecture is given by a native speaker who uses displays, short themes, or whatever is flexible and encourages students to use target language.
49) Lectures with accompanying slides.
50) The department encourages foreign travel.

51) The teacher uses films, music, magazines and other materials which are
aimed at contemporizing subject, and
trying to draw out a realistic and
"live" approach.
52) Intermediate and advanced students
help teach beginning students.
53) An instructional team has been established with one faculty-level instructor, one teaching assistant (French
native speaker), one student tutor
(Haitian) for 25-30 students in a
multi-level group.
54) The department utilizes programmed
instruction in all first year classes.
55) Establishment of a language club with
major meetings once a month.
56) College language students go to
neighboring high schools and talk to
high school students.
57) The department is preparing a brochure
on foreign languages at the institution.
58) There are individual readings one day
a week when each student reads according to his own ability.
59) One or two days a week there is
conversation at a language table.
60) The language course is not programmed
with the language major in mind.
61) Individual attention is given to students with oral participation sometimes directed by students.
62) The department is trying to implement
self-pacing.
63) The teacher tries to consider student's
goals and background in the selection
and presentation of materials.
64) The department gives goal options (A,
B, C basic achievement totals) with a
type of premium smorgasbord for the

students who want *A*'s and *B*'s.
65) Students attend German theater or German films.
66) Classes celebrate traditional holidays with programs, films, lectures.
67) The teacher requests and uses materials from embassies.
68) Taped lessons on cassettes are placed in the library so that students can listen to material either at the library or at home.
69) In elementary German students present dialogs to the class as soon as they are memorized; they can repeat dialogs if the memorization is unsatisfactory; these dialogs are not graded; therefore, students can work at their own pace.
70) The techniques and methods utilized are those shown in a booklet put out by the State Department of Education.
71) As aides the teacher uses local high school language students.
72) The department uses native speakers.
73) Foreign dinners are organized.
See also L 15, 17, 18, 20.

N. WHAT IS THE ADMINISTRATION DOING TO IMPROVE FOREIGN LANGUAGE CURRICULA OR TO HELP INCREASE FOREIGN LANGUAGE ENROLLMENT?

1) Administration allows for the teaching of second-year courses.
2) It recommends that all education majors take Spanish to help their employment chances in areas of Spanish-speaking people.
3) Administration does nothing.
4) It allows flexibility in setting up programs.

5) Administration readily helps department to obtain materials and equipment.
6) Administration is eager to set up
   ethnic and cultural courses because
   administrators want to enroll in such
   courses.
7) Administration has increased departmental budget.
8) Administration sends teachers to language meetings at school expense.
9) Learning Resource Center secures audio-
   visual materials, books and periodicals.
10) Administration doesn't do much.
11) Counselors urge good students to enroll
    in foreign languages.
12) Administration is willing to listen to
    suggestions for improvement from
    foreign language department.
13) Administration supports complete
    foreign language program.
14) Administration provides all materials
    and equipment requested to develop
    foreign language program.
15) Counselors and public relations have
    done much to attract students to
    foreign language programs.
16) Administration and department are
    exploring possibility of going beyond
    basic grammar courses into courses in
    literature and civilization (possibly
    implemented in Fall of 1972).
17) Administration has furnished busses for
    trips to the border, but students and
    faculty have had to pay own expenses.
18) Administration has not supplied
    sufficient classroom space.
19) Administration is considering foreign
    language as a graduation requirement
    for the A.A. degree.
20) Administration has increased the basic
    courses from three hours of credit to

167

five hours of credit.

21) In the Fall the administration will approve intermediate reading grammar courses in Spanish and French.

22) Department will be offering short courses in languages for tourists in order to serve community and area needs.

23) Administration has approved the establishment of a language club.

24) Administration is sympathetic, but state higher education requirements tend to eliminate courses with small enrollments (this school is a university branch).

25) Administration is considering the hiring of a full-time instructor.

26) Administration gives students the option of substituting foreign language for the speech requirement and still fulfill graduation requirements.

27) Teachers are encouraged to improve themselves but are not financially remunerated if they do so.

28) Administration will give "prime time" to foreign languages when drawing up class schedules.

29) Administration cooperates in preparation of brochures.

30) Administration does not cancel small foreign language classes (six or less) but would do so in other disciplines.

31) Administration keeps foreign language program open-ended and allows department to experiment with techniques and books.

32) Administration makes attempts to sell foreign language to students and public.

33) Administration encourages new courses.

34) Administration encourages teach teaching with other disciplines (government,

history, social studies, mathematics, science).
35) More publicity is being sent out to patrons in the district.
36) Administration is adverse to small classes but permits foreign language staff to teach advanced classes of one, two, three, or four students; but administration does not pay staff for teaching these classes.
37) Administration has given *carte blanche* in the operation of the foreign language department and has approved third-level courses in French and German for sophomores who have completed second-level courses as freshmen.
38) Administration has given teacher all help teacher has requested.
39) Administration of one college is cooperating with another college in acquiring a language laboratory. Then each school will offer certain languages not offered by the other with subsequent exchange of students.
40) Advisors are told to push foreign languages.
41) Administration has removed some outside duties of the teacher (teaching journalism classes) so he can concentrate more on foreign language teaching.
42) Administration is receptive to suggestions but will not spend money on courses unless enrollment is high.
43) Administration has cooperated in the establishment of interterm programs in Mexico, Argentina, and Germany.
44) There is much emphasis on being genuinely interested in some area of the world besides our own.

45) Administration encourages departments to innovate, to formulate behavioral objectives.
46) Administration pushes Spanish conversation as fulfilling humanities requirement.
47) Department will be allowed to participate in the recruiting of students.
48) Administration is investigating ways to increase foreign language enrollment.
49) Administration is reducing department size by a half instructor in spite of a foreign language enrollment increase in order to compensate for losses elsewhere in college.
50) Division is reassessing its goals.
51) Administration is establishing procedures for continuous enrollment.
52) Administration is considering foreign language as one of the core curriculum requirements.
53) Administration has helped in the acquiring of a French teaching assistant.
54) Administration helped secure a foreign language consultant for two months in 1970-1971 in French; in 1971-1972, a consultant in Spanish and Latin American studies will be retained for two months.
55) Teacher isn't aware of any administration help.
56) Administration is attempting to add more instructors.
57) Administration and the curriculum committee allowed foreign language department to revamp its entire curricula to the point where students in this college can obtain 21 hours of credit in French, and 22 hours of

credit in German in four semesters.

58) Foreign language department has been given the right to allow students who already speak a foreign language to bypass basic courses and to go immediately into advanced courses.

59) Department has been able to obtain films, filmstrips, slides outside of departmental budget (audio-visual committee funds) and, in addition, has a budget for miscellaneous and unexpected wants.

60) Administration has allowed the department to establish a bilingual secretarial course.

61) College has discontinued second-year language courses. The teacher has been able to teach in another discipline, otherwise he would probably be out of a job.

62) Administration is not doing anything that is significant.

11. THE STATUS OF FOREIGN LANGUAGES IN JUNIOR COLLEGES IN ILLINOIS, 1971

SISTER MARY CELESTE
Office of the Superintendent of Public Instruction
Springfield, Illinois

In order to have specific information on what was happening to foreign language education in Illinois a state-wide survey was conducted on the status of foreign languages under the auspices of the Department of Foreign Languages, Instruction and Curriculum Section, Office of the Superintendent of Public Instruction. On October 15, 1971, a questionnaire was sent to Illinois public, parochial, and private schools. A separate survey was mailed on November 15, 1971, to all Illinois junior colleges, liberal arts colleges and universities.

The information which follows is from *The Status of Foreign Language Education in Illinois. A Report of the State-Wide Survey, 1971* distributed by the Instruction and Curriculum Section of the Office of the Superintendent of Public Instruction, Springfield, Illinois.

31 Junior Colleges that Participated in the Survey

Belleville Area College
Carl Sandburg College
College of DuPage
Danville Junior College
Elgin Community College
Felician College
Highland Community College
John A. Logan College
Joliet Junior College
Kaskaskia College
Kendall College
Kishwaukee College
Lewis & Clark Community College
Lincoln Land College
Lincoln Trail College
Loop College
Malcolm X College
Mayfair City College of Chicago
McHenry County College
Oakton Community College
Olney Central College
Parkland College
Prairie State College
Robert Morris College
Sauk Valley College
Shawnee Community College
Southwest College
Spoon River College
Springfield College
Triton College
Wabash Valley College
Waubonsee Community College
Wright Junior College

A summary of the projections for the next two years in junior colleges shows some plan to introduce Polish, Russian, and German into

the curriculum. Others anticipate continuous
growth in foreign languages, while some hope
to develop their current offerings by adding
more advanced courses. One junior college
reports more demand than staff and facilities
can handle. Another projects increased enrollment and interdisciplinary programs.
Some anticipate no changes and hope to continue their offerings.

Three junior colleges reported study
abroad programs in France, Germany and Spain,
and one in Mexico during the semester interim.

Some of the statistics from the junior
college survey are summarized below.

CHART I
STUDENT ENROLLMENT BY LANGUAGES
IN JUNIOR COLLEGES
(31 participating institutions)

LANGUAGES	FALL 1970	FALL 1971
French	1,551	1,392
German	1,123	1,112
Greek	--	30
Italian	292	318
Latin	--	--
Russian	164	177
Spanish	2,444	2,360
Hebrew	75	90
Japanese	50	60
TOTAL	5,699	5,619

CHART II
STUDENT ENROLLMENT BY MAJORS
IN JUNIOR COLLEGES

LANGUAGES	FALL 1970	FALL 1971
French	1	11
German	--	1
Greek	--	1
Italian	--	--
Latin	--	--
Russian	--	--
Spanish	14	30
Portuguese	--	--
Hebrew	--	--
Japanese	--	--
TOTAL	15	43

CHART III
FOREIGN LANGUAGE PROGRAMS
IN JUNIOR COLLEGES

LANGUAGES	JUNIOR COLLEGES
French	30
German	22
Italian	4
Latin	--
Russian	5
Spanish	31
Modern Hebrew	1
Japanese	1
Polish	1
Swahili	1
TOTAL	96

CHART IV
GENERAL INFORMATION FOR JUNIOR COLLEGES

		Junior Colleges
Total Student Enrollment Fall 1971		28,226
Foreign Language Enrollment Fall 1971		5,619
Entrance Requirement	YES	4
	NO	29
Advanced Placement Program	YES	21
	NO	9
Teacher Training Program	YES	1
	NO	32
Programs Emphasize Language	YES	16
Per Se	NO	12
Interdisciplinary Programs	YES	5
	NO	26
Area Studies Program	YES	5
	NO	26

12. ENGLISH AS A SECOND LANGUAGE IN ILLINOIS JUNIOR AND COMMUNITY COLLEGE

MARY A. HUSSEY
University of Illinois

This report is based upon information accumulated by means of a telephone survey plus a few personal interviews--both conducted by six different persons. Hence, a certain lack of uniformity in the resulting answers became evident when the findings were assembled and studied to produce a hopefully useful summary. Fifty-one institutions were on the list, but no responses were elicited from four.

DIFFERENCES BETWEEN FOREIGN LANGUAGE TEACHING AND TEACHING ENGLISH AS A SECOND LANGUAGE

Since this is one small unit in a report primarily concerned with FL teaching, some differences should be pointed out which exist between FL programs and ESL programs.

1) *Student population*. The enrollment of
non-native speakers of English in the community colleges, except in certain areas where
migrants and immigrants are served, is so
small that in most cases the schools have not
felt a need to provide special instruction in
English for these students. It is true that
in some instances lack of funds is the reason
for the failure to set up ESL classes; and in
others perhaps a lack of recognition of the
problem is the reason. At any rate, the
foreign students with a language handicap
are, in many of these schools, placed in
developmental sections of English along with
the native English speakers and second dialect
students -if any- who need corrective work
and are handled on a tutorial basis if the
regular classroom program is not sufficient.

2) *Motivation, goals, proficiency and
needs*. The regularly enrolled students in
community colleges, as well as migrant and
immigrant students enrolled in both day and
night classes, have a more urgent purpose
than do the students in FL classes. The
regular college students must, within a
relatively short period of time, learn
English well enough to pursue academic
courses in their curricula; and the migrant
and other FL background enrollees are under
pressure to acquire a facility in the language that will enable them to get and hold
jobs.

3) *Attitudes*. All regularly enrolled
students in the community colleges will probably have more or less the same attitudes
toward the classroom environment -excepting
those variations resulting from cultural
differences- as do American students taking

178

FL courses. But for the migrant and immigrant students, who comprise the majority of
ESL students enrolled in the community colleges, particularly in the urban areas, this
familiar feeling of being in an environment
of classrooms, teachers, textbooks, etc.,
may not be present. Among the immigrant
groups there may be persons who have lived in
the U.S. for many years but who for various
reasons have not developed facility in
English. For all of these groups of FL background it would appear, then, that special
provision should be made to provide them with
English language instruction.

INTERRELATIONSHIPS BETWEEN FL TEACHING AND
ESL TEACHING

    1) *Part-time FL and ESL teachers.* There
may well be differences in addition to those
mentioned above, but at the same time certain
bonds are growing between FL teaching and ESL
teaching in the community colleges. One is
that, in lieu of a trained ESL teacher,
foreign language teachers are sometimes
called upon to teach English on a part-time
basis to the non-native speakers of English
in the student body.

    2) *TESL in the FL teachers' curricula.*
As a result of this, some colleges and
universities require, or at least give credit
for, courses in TESL in the curricula for
future FL teachers.

INNOVATIONS

    1) *Inter-institutional cooperation.* One
of the recent trends in ESL -though not
unique to ESL- is the development of inter-
institutional cooperation. In some instances,

179

this consists of a rather closely knit combination of schools, such as MONACEP (Maine, Oakton, Niles Adult and Continuing Education Program), in which the participants feel that all sorts of educational problems are better handled and that richer curricula can be offered than otherwise would be possible. In other cases, cooperation is based on an internship program, such as exists between Malcolm X College and the Chicago Circle campus of the University of Illinois, and also between Malcolm X and the University of Massachusetts.

In fact, the internship program itself is a strong manifestation of an awakening to the various possibilities in TESL. Triton College and the Division of English as a Second Language at the University of Illinois at Urbana are currently discussing and planning an internship at Triton to begin in September, 1972. The two U. of I. internees who will be teaching at Triton nine hours a week each will be enrolled in a special extension seminar course in TESL. This "field-oriented" course, which offers both graduate and undergraduate credit, will include practical applications to the real situations in which the trainees are involved, and will focus special attention upon linguistic, social, and psychological aspects of communicative competence for cross-cultural interaction and upon pedagogical procedures and materials for developing this competence. In other words, the aim is a pooling of academic expertise, practical experience, and original classroom materials that will provide on-going enrichment for all participants.

2) *PLATO*. PLATO is another recently explored device for teaching ESL. An experiment with PLATO lessons is now being carried
on by the Division of English as a Second
Language of the Urbana campus of the University of Illinois. If present plans materi-
alize, PLATO terminals will be established
by the fall of 1972 in the following community colleges in the City Colleges of Chicago
system: Malcolm X, Kennedy-King, Wright, the
Skills Center, and Loop. In addition to ESL
lessons, ESD lessons will be available if an
NSF grant at present being sought is granted.

3) *Telephone lessons*. Lessons in ESL via
telephone are available in the State of
Illinois from the Division of English as a
Second Language (laboratory) at the University of Illinois, Urbana; Tel: 217-333-3788.

SPECIAL PROGRAMS IN ESL IN ILLINOIS

Fifteen schools in the group contacted
have special courses in ESL, these varying
from one section to the multi-level programs
in some of the metropolitan junior colleges.
A brief description of the courses offered
by four different schools with a large enrollment follows. Sufficient details about
other programs are not immediately available.

1) *Loop College (City Colleges of
Chicago)*. Loop offers two programs: (1) a
full-time international student program for
those with visas, and (2) a part-time program for immigrants. In the first program
there are two sections, each with an enrollment of twenty-five students, their placement being determined by the Michigan ELI
objective tests and by a composition and an
oral interview. Any of these students who

181

test over 75 may take two courses (mathematics and science) in addition to the English course(s). The courses that a student takes in this plan are followed by regular Rhetoric for American students, the ESL courses having stressed reading and composition. The second program consists of fifteen sections, each meeting twice a week for two hours each time. *English 900* is the text. These students are placed on the basis of an oral interview. Most of the sections meet in the evening; however, two meet in the morning and two in the early afternoon. The sections have twenty-five to thirty students each, some of whom have not completed high school.

2) *Central YMCA Community College (Chicago, Illinois).* This school offers intensive English to about three hundred students per semester, meeting sixteen hours per week for sixteen weeks. At the low level two of the University of Michigan's English Language Institute's textbooks are used: *English Sentence Structure* and *English Pattern Practice*. Jean Praninskas' *Rapid Review of English Grammar* is used at the intermediate level; and a variety of texts is used at the upper level, such as *Developing Reading Efficiency* by Miller, and the Harris reading and word book. The ESL classes are partly staffed by returning Peace Corps participants.

3) *Triton College (River Grove, Illinois).* Triton has an extensive offering in ESL, with three levels of classes meeting three hours per week for twelve weeks. The enrollment in these courses runs from two to three hundred per semester, requiring about twenty sections. The textbooks are the Dixon series and the *Reader's Digest* for ESL, plus others.

182

As in many schools, the ESL teachers are part-time.

4) *Illinois Central College (East Peoria)*. The college is planning to offer a Conversational English course for migrant workers at Princeville, Illinois. The primary objective is to introduce migrant workers to the basic English required for minimal efficiency at work and in the community.

SOME STATISTICS

1) *Number of foreign students enrolled.* Six of the community colleges contacted have no foreign student population--and apparently seldom, if ever, do. Strangely enough, foreign students are never admitted to two of the schools. At the other extreme, four of the institutions serve from 200 to 350 per semester, some on the intensive plan. One school has an erratic enrollment ranging from fifteen in the academic year to fifty in the summer session, and another has from ten to twenty. The others have from five to ten.

2) *Interest in ESL and ESD (English as a Second Dialect)*. Only fourteen schools indicated a lack of interest in, or recognition of, the ESL problem. These were institutions with a light enrollment (5-10) or none, and the feeling seemed to be that they were taking care of their problem adequately by placing those students in developmental sections or labs, along with native speakers with low test scores or dialect problems, and/or by tutoring, or in some cases, by simply placing them in the regular classes with native speakers of English. One school reported that their entire foreign student population came from

one country and that all were proficient
enough in English to carry a full load of
academic work without further study of the
language. This is, of course, a highly unusual situation.

Only two of the schools provide special
help for second dialect students, although
one is currently planning an ESD program and
one said that 20% of the enrolled students
had dialect problems but that there is no
provision for them; all the others disclaim-
ed the presence of ESD on their campuses.
However, three schools have, or have had,
courses in black literature or black social
studies.

3) *Interest in ESL centers, conferences,
and professional organizations.* A third of
the schools indicated interest in area conferences and centers, and in professional
organizations, though the interviewers got
the idea that their attendance at national
conferences would probably not be heavy,
probably because of lack of funds.

4) *Financial problems.* Actually only
three schools gave lack of money as a serious
reason for offering no special English courses
for foreign students. Two said that if the
need arose, funds would probably be provided.
But most of those not having ESL programs
felt that the main reason was lack of need--
therefore lack of interest.

5) *Needs expressed.* In addition to the
general need for TESL-trained teachers -even
where complex ESL programs are in use- a need
for teaching materials and new tests were expressed by two schools. The materials and

the tests would apparently be used by the present teaching staff, though not TESL-trained.

6) *Presence of special TESL-trained staff.* Aside from the several Chicago area schools with a heavy enrollment and elaborate programs, only three TESL-trained teachers were mentioned in the other colleges.

13. STUDENT INTERESTS IN FOREIGN LANGUAGE PROGRAMS

RAYMOND ARCHER and DANIEL O'ROURKE
Prairie State College
Chicago Heights, Illinois

The Foreign Language Department of Prairie
State College in Chicago Heights, Illinois,
recently conducted a survey in order to
determine why enrollment is low in foreign
language courses. Questionnaires were distributed to students registering for the
Spring semester in 1972, and responses were
obtained from 402 students. Since a total
of about 3800 persons registered, our sampling is rather small; it is, however, random,
and we hope it is representative of the general feelings of students at Prairie State.

Our questionnaire consisted of 32 statements. Participants were asked to indicate
on an IBM sheet whether they A) strongly
agreed, B) agreed, C) were neutral, D) disagreed, or E) strongly disagreed with each
statement. Results were tabulated by the
Data Processing Service at Prairie State

186

College. A copy of the questionnaire is included here as an appendix. In the following report, the percentages of "strongly agree" and "agree", as well as those of "disagree" and "strongly disagree" are combined in order to present the general picture more simply to the reader. We found that positive versus negative responses were important, but degrees of feeling within the two attitudes were not generally significant.

Response to items 1 and 7 indicate a very strong interest in learning to speak and comprehend a foreign language (72%) or use the language in a practical way (65%). Items 17 and 27 further substantiate the interest in conversation in first and second year courses (59% and 68% respectively). There is a strong interest in the study of literature: 56% favor attaining a literary and intellectual background through foreign language study (item 4), 40% favor reading literature in the foreign language in first year courses (item 19) and 50% (item 28) in second year courses.

Students are far from adverse to the study of grammar: 41% (item 2) hope to learn to understand English better through foreign language study, and 42% (item 16) want intensive grammar study in first year, while 49% (item 26) want it in second year. Only 24% (item 13) felt that there was too much emphasis on grammar in foreign language study. There is considerable interest in readings on general topics at both levels: 42% in first year (item 20) and 50% in second year (item 29). There is great interest in the study of a foreign land and culture (61% in item 5), the country and its people (55% in item 22), and in acquiring the tools for

understanding a foreign land (54% in item 6).
About 44% of the respondants were interested
in hearing records and seeing films and
slides (items 23, 24, and 25) in elementary
courses, and 50% would like to read newspapers and magazines in the intermediate
courses (item 30).

37% of the students understand that they
may need to fulfill a language requirement
eventually (item 3), though 24% do not expect
to face such a requirement. Only 27% are
interested in studying purely linguistic
questions (item 18), but 34% would like to
study foreign literature in translation in
elementary courses (item 21), and 39% would
like to do so in the intermediate courses
(item 31). 40% would like to do some independent study with their instructor at the
intermediate level (item 32).

We can safely conclude from the above
data that students at Prairie State College
are not particularly hostile to foreign language study. They have not been prejudiced
against it in high school (item 11), nor do
they have strong objections to the methods
currently being used. They favor the study
of grammar, conversation, culture and literature. Only a few felt that there was too
much emphasis on conversation (10% in item 14)
or reading (12% in item 15). 21% indicated
that they could not take a language course at
the time it was offered, but 30% indicated
that they had no scheduling difficulty
(item 9). 33% felt that language study had
no practical value for them, but 27% felt
that it did (item 10). 26% thought that
foreign language courses were more difficult
than other subjects, but 35% felt that they
were not more difficult (item 12). There is

clearly a large number of students at
Prairie State College - perhaps as many as
25% of the population - who express strong
approval of and interest in foreign language
study, but only about 2.2% of the student
body actually registers for foreign language
courses. The explanation is probably to be
found in item 8, "I am presently committed
to satisfying other requirements and/or
interests," a statement which received a
resounding 72% agreement.

QUESTIONNAIRE FOR FOREIGN LANGUAGE COURSES AT PRAIRIE STATE COLLEGE

The Foreign Language Department is interested
in evaluating its present program, and the
views of students are important in establishing the kinds of change which may be needed.
It would be helpful to us if you would answer
each of the following questions accordingly:
A) Strongly agree; B) Agree; C) Neutral;
D) Disagree; E) Strongly disagree.

Why study a foreign language?

1. Learn to speak and comprehend the foreign
   language.
2. Gain a better understanding of English
   usage and grammar.
3. Fulfill a requirement.
4. Gain a literary and intellectual background.
5. Gain a knowledge of a foreign land and
   its customs.
6. Provides necessary tools for understanding a foreign land in the context of a
   foreign language.
7. Use the language in a practical way, that
   is, for professional use (social worker,
   business, police work, hospital work,
   nurse, doctor, etc.)

Why aren't you taking a foreign language
course at present?

8. I am presently committed to satisfying other requirements and/or interests.
9. I cannot take it at the time offered.
10. It has no practical value in my course of study.
11. I didn't like it in high school.
12. A foreign language is probably more difficult than most other subjects.
13. There is too much emphasis on grammar.
14. There is too much emphasis on conversation.
15. There is too much emphasis on reading.

What do you want from elementary foreign
language courses?

16. Thorough study of grammar, syntax and vocabulary.
17. Emphasis on conversation.
18. Discussion of linguistic questions (comparisons and contrasts).
19. Readings of foreign literature (stories, plays, novels).
20. Readings on general topics (current events, history, etc.)
21. Readings of literature in English translations.
22. Information on the country and its people.
23. Viewing foreign films.
24. Listening to records of foreign songs, plays and music.
25. Slides to show the country, its life, art and tourist attractions.

What do you want from intermediate foreign
language courses?

26. Intensive study of grammar, vocabulary and problems of translation.

27. Develop fluency in conversation.
28. Readings of foreign literature (stories, plays, novels).
29. Readings on general topics (current events, history, etc.)
30. Reading foreign newspapers and magazines.
31. Readings of literature in English translations.
32. The opportunity to do some independent study with my instructor, in association with regular class sessions.

14. A SURVEY OF STUDENT ATTITUDES TOWARD ELEMENTARY AND INTERMEDIATE FRENCH COURSES AT THE UNIVERSITY OF ILLINOIS

PAULETTE PELC and SHARON SAUDER
University of Illinois

In recent years, the status of foreign language study has become the subject of much controversy. Its relevance has been continually challenged both by educators and students who feel that the study of foreign language is neither related to nor purposeful in their specific disciplines. Opposition to the foreign language requirement has grown to such an extent that many colleges and universities have been pressured to abolish such required courses. During the past year the motion to abolish the foreign language requirement, made on the assumption that it is irrelevant, was defeated at the University of Illinois.

Our contention is that foreign language study need not be considered an irrelevant, burdensome, or useless activity. Today's

192

student is seemingly more active, more aware, and more involved in a variety of activities than his predecessors. In view of its flexible character, it should be possible for a foreign language program to assimilate this multiplicity of student interests into a more relevant content. Perhaps the image of the foreign language course will become more appealing to a greater number of students when they find that it is receptive to their concerns.

In view of this need for change, we became interested in finding out where student interests lie, how students in the elementary stages of study feel about a foreign language (in this case French), and whether, as their study progresses, their attitudes change and they feel an increasing need to incorporate their interests into the foreign language course.

This survey was administered to 141 randomly selected students presently enrolled in elementary and intermediate French courses in the 101 through 104 levels at the University of Illinois, sampling approximately 35 students from each course level. The questionnaires were distributed by the instructors in each section, and the students were informed that all answers would remain anonymous.

Initially, the survey was designed to assess student interests and to see if a significant contrast in interests and attitudes would be expressed by the students in the various levels. We felt the questionnaire might serve to point out a developing trend of dissatisfaction among students who had progressed to the 104 level and that this trend would reflect their broadening interests, causing a change in attitudes toward their French courses and toward foreign language study in general. We also felt that such a change (or difference in attitudes expressed by students in the various levels) would represent not only the students' expanding interests and increased involvement in the university environment, but also their growing away as individuals from a dependency on structure and the development of a more aggressively expressed need (or demand) to see these interests made relevant in the foreign language classroom. However, in addition to what we had hoped to assess, we found that the results also had many other implications, some of which are more pertinent or interesting as they expand on our initial objectives.

The format of the questionnaire was as follows (see sample questionnaire included in the report):

1) Demographic information such as age, sex, year in school. (Questions 1-9).
2) General interests and involvement in activities. (Questions 10 and 11).
3) Why students take foreign language courses. (Questions 12-14).
4) Would students take a foreign language if not required? (Questions 15 and 18).
5) Do students have confidence that they will be able to use French with any degree of facility? (Question 17).
6) How students rate the importance of foreign language courses as compared with other subjects. (Question 19).
7) Student evaluation of course content and method--preferences and changes desired. (Question 19).

8) Learning styles. (Questions 24 and 25).
9) How much at ease do students feel in using
   language skills in the classroom?
   (Questions 26-28).

Responses were cross-sorted by computer
according to the following:

1) General overall response (141 students).
2) Level of study: 101 (35), 102 (35),
   103 (33), 104 (38).
3) Sex: 60 males (44%) and 76 females (55%).
4) Age

Other factors considered were the number of
years of study of French, the grade received
in French in the previous semester of study,
the number taking the Pass/Fail option (104
only), the year in school, and the major area
of study.

    A numerical scale (4-3-2-1) was used by
students in recording responses, with 4 having the highest value and indicating the
most emphatic response (degree of importance,
interest, etc.). Several yes/no questions
were included where 1 = yes and 2 - no.

INTEREST AND INVOLVEMENT

    The question concerning interest (number
10) was placed at the beginning of the
questionnaire so as first to elicit interests
of a general nature, to be followed later by
question 23 which indicates the degree to
which students would like some of these interests to be related more specifically to
their study of French.

    The total response of all 141 students
to question 10 showed the greatest interest

195

in current affairs (77%), followed by literature (68%), and the arts (58%). The 101
group responded with the same hierarchy of
interest ratings while in the 104 group,
interest in politics increased sharply as
compared to 101 (46% to 66%). It was also
interesting to note that all groups rated
current affairs very highly and literature
and the arts generally ranked second and
third. As one might expect, male students
ranked sciences as one of their three main
interests (66%) but sciences ranked even
higher among those students 22 and older
(75%).

Interest in foreign languages generally
received one of the lower ratings. Showing
the most interest in FLs was the 18-year-old
group (51%), followed by the 101 group and
female students (each with 45%). There was
a noticeable difference in the percentage
between the 101 and 104 groups as it decreased markedly from 45% in 101 to 26% in 104.
This drop in interest might be attributed to
an increasing dissatisfaction with course
content, to the number of 104 students elect-
ing the Pass/Fail option (19 or half of the
104 group surveyed) who are perhaps no longer
as interested as other students, and for the
majority of students to a decrease of interest in foreign language study as they near
the completion of the foreign language
requirement. It may also be due to unpleas-
and experiences in the language-learning
situation or to a loss of motivation, possibly as a result of poor grades received in
prior French courses, poor teacher/student
rapport, or because of the failure of the
foreign language course to respond to their
personal interests. (All the 104 students
in the survey were in general 104 classes,

not those with specialized curricula. See
Action Report by W. M. Rivers.)

Question 11 was intended to test whether
students were actively involved in those
areas in which they had expressed interest.
Students were generally most involved in
environmental concerns. Most areas of
activity corresponded to general areas of
interest, although interests were consistently rated much higher than actual involvement.
Once again, the 104 group was significantly
more active in the area of politics than was
the 101 group (45% to 20%). It would seem
that as a result of time spent in the University environment, the students tend to develop or acquire more political awareness.

COURSE EVALUATION AND PREFERENCES

In question 16 the 104 level students
and males showed a marked preference for a
French culture course rather than a purely
language oriented course. With other groups
there was no significant preference.

All groups felt that students should have
a greater say in determining the content and
methods of the foreign language course. However, at least 50% in all groups showed satisfaction with the course content and the
teaching methods employed. The group expressing the most dissatisfaction was the 104
group (47%-content and 45%-methods).

The response to question 23 showed that
a large percentage of students in all groups
were interested in the incorporation of more
cultural information. Consistent with the
contrasts in political interest and involvement between the 101 and 104 groups that we

197

have already indicated, the 104 students expressed a desire for more discussion of controversial issues (social/political questions) in the classroom (66%), as compared with 49% for 101 students. Curiously, those in the 22 and older group indicated almost no interest in this area. Generally, the groups were equally divided as to whether they wanted more study of literature.

The majority in all groups desired more reading of French magazines and newspapers (this being a reflection of the great interest shown by all groups in current affairs).

Emphatically negative response (87% opposed) came from all groups when asked if they desired more listening practice in the language lab, while approximately 35% desired more listening practice in class.

WHY STUDENTS TAKE A FOREIGN LANGUAGE

Question 13 showed that 69% of the students were taking a foreign language because it was required. It is interesting to note that 84% of the students in 104 as opposed to 49% in 101 listed the foreign language requirement as their reason for taking a foreign language. When asked why they specifically chose to study French (question 14), the most frequently occurring response in all groups was personal interest.

In question 12 students were asked to indicate how important they thought parents, friends, teachers, society, and they themselves considered language study to be. Teachers, as might be expected, received the highest overall rating (71%). Of the students themselves 51% felt that language study was of importance. It seemed quite unusual, however, that of these students only 9% felt their peer group regarded language study as being important. Perhaps these students are exceptionally individualistic and are not influenced by their friends' opinions, perhaps they have misjudged the attitudes of their friends, or perhaps they were not being completely honest and were responding in this case as they felt they *should*. Discrepancies between the 101 and 104 groups were again evident, 101 students generally feeling that language study was more important (69%) than did the 104 students (42%), with a similar difference observable when they were rating their friends' feelings (27% and 11% respectively).

Reasons other than the requirement which seemed to have a significant influence on the students' choice to study a foreign language were the desire to increase cultural awareness (38% overall) and interest in language for travel purposes (47% overall).

It was found that 45% of all the students would take a foreign language even if not required to do so. This percentage was highest in the 101, female, and 22 and older groups. The 104 group showed the least favorable response with 61% indicating they would not take a foreign language if it were not required.

When asked to rate their foreign language course in comparison with other courses they were taking, none of the students in the 104 group rated their French course as most important (47% said it was the least important). In the 101 group, 11% rated it as the most important and 37% least important.

Questions 24 and 25 relate to the individual learning styles of the students. Generally, students felt they learned best in a group of 5 to 10 students (which in some cases was the size of their class anyway). This choice received the greatest response in every group except for those 22 and older who preferred a group of 2-3 students. Few indicated they learned best either alone or in a regular sized class (15-20 students).

The greatest variance in response to question 25 was found in the age groups. The younger students (age 18) indicated a 52% preference for a regular classroom situation while only 17% of those 22 and older preferred that situation.

EASE OF USE OF LANGUAGE SKILLS

Overall, students felt the least comfortable in using speaking skills (76% total, with no group under 72%). The 104 students felt only slightly more comfortable in speaking in the foreign language than did students in 101 (74% uneasy in 104 and 80% uneasy in 101). It might have been expected that the 104 students would have acquired more confidence or assurance as their familiarity with the language increased. This degree of uneasiness would seem to indicate some failing or inadequacy in the elementary foreign language program to provide the kind of situation and practice necessary to develop these skills since it seems unlikely that such a strong feeling of uneasiness could be explained merely in terms of student personalities.

It was found (question 27) that in general, 42% of the students felt uneasy or reluctant to participate in class because of the fear of making mistakes or of sounding ridiculous. Of the different groups, 104 students felt the most uneasy (50%) as did those in the 22 and older group (50%). Again, the greatest degree of uneasiness was expressed by 104 students, with 24% as compared with 11% for 101 students.

Most students (70%) blamed themselves for their uneasiness (question 28); however, the 104 group tended to place more responsibility on both teachers (21%) and other students (16%). Perhaps these students feel a greater need to rationalize their own lack of interest or motivation by blaming others for their "predicament."

Of those 104 students who elected to take the course on the Pass/Fail option, 42% said they would take a foreign language even if not required. There seemed to be little significant variation between 104 Pass/Fail responses and those of the regular 104 group.

CONCLUSION

Overall, results of the survey indicated that 39% of the 141 students participating felt that they would be able to use French with some degree of facility (question 17) indicating that the introductory French language program is relatively adequate. However, the trend of response to this question from the 101 through 104 levels seems to make the figure less encouraging. In the 101

group the percentage of students who felt
they would be able to use French with a
degree of facility was 51%; this percentage
decreased in each subsequent course to 35%
of 104 students. This seems to support our
previously mentioned findings that 104 students displayed the most dissatisfaction
both with course content and methods of
teaching, the most desire to see their
interests incorporated into classroom discussion, and the most uneasiness and reluc-
tance to use their oral skills in the classroom situation.

The results we have found are by no
means comprehensive or conclusive, yet, in
developing a basic foreign language program
or in reconsidering already established
programs, an attempt should surely be made
to elicit student opinions and identify student interests. Information gathered in
such surveys as this can prove valuable in
both the reevaluation and the restructuring
of foreign language programs so as to
coordinate student interests with course
structure and content. Student learning
styles must also be considered if we are to
create the most motivating materials and
present them in the most comfortable learning
situation.

QUESTIONNAIRE ON STUDENT INTERESTS

We would appreciate your help and cooperation
in completing the following survey. Please
do not put your name on this sheet as the
survey is to be completely anonymous and
responses will in no way affect your grade.
Please answer the following questions as

honestly as possible. Circle or fill in the
most appropriate answer. Thank you.

1) Course number: 101   102   103   104
2) If 104, are you taking it pass/fail?
                                yes   no
3) Sex   M   F
4) Age_____
5) Class in school. Fr So Jr Sr Grad
6) Major_____
7) Minor_____
8) What grade did you receive in French last
   semester? A   B   C   D   E
9) How long have you studied French?
   1 yr.   2   3   4   5
10) Rate the following as to the degree of
    importance--the higher the number, the
    greater the importance.
    I am interested in:
      literature   4   3   2   1
      sciences   4   3   2   1
      politics   4   3   2   1
      current affairs   4   3   2   1
      student affairs   4   3   2   1
      history   4   3   2   1
      arts   4   3   2   1
      this community   4   3   2   1
      foreign languages   4   3   2   1
      other (please specify)_____
11) I am actively involved in:
      literary activities   4   3   2   1
      science related activities 4   3   2   1
      politics   4   3   2   1
      student affairs   4   3   2   1
      the arts   4   3   2   1
      community affairs (local)   4   3   2   1
      environmental concerns   4   3   2   1
12) How important do you think the following
    people feel language study is?
      parents   4   3   2   1
      friends   4   3   2   1

```
           teachers                  4  3  2  1
           society                   4  3  2  1
           you                       4  3  2  1
13) List the degree of importance each of
    the following had in your studying a
    foreign language.
       was a requirement             4  3  2  1
       useful for research in my
          field                      4  3  2  1
       to broaden cultural back-
          ground and learn more
          of the people and         4  3  2  1
          literature of the country
       for travel                    4  3  2  1
       useful in my future
          vocation                   4  3  2  1
       communicating with those
          speaking the language      4  3  2  1
       seemed like a cool thing
          to do                      4  3  2  1
14) List the degree to which each of the
    following influenced your choice in
    selecting French.
       parents                       4  3  2  1
       friends                       4  3  2  1
       other relatives               4  3  2  1
       teachers                      4  3  2  1
       personal interest             4  3  2  1
       other (please specify)_____
15) Would you take a foreign language if it
    were not required?          yes    no
16) Would you prefer taking French culture
    to French language if the option were
    available?                  yes    no
17) Do you think you will ever
    be able to use French with
    any degree of facility?      4  3  2  1
18) Do you intend to take French
    courses after 104?          yes    no
19) How would you rate the importance of
    your language course in comparison to
```

204

the other courses you are taking? (Use
the lowest number to indicate the most
important.)   4 3 2 1
20) Do you think that students should have a
    greater say in the content and methods
    concerning foreign language study?
                                    yes   no
21) Are you satisfied with the content of
    this course?   yes   no
22) Are you satisfied with the way this
    course is taught?   yes   no
23) I would prefer:
      more speaking in French   4 3 2 1
      more info. on France and
        French people   4 3 2 1
      more discussion on contro-
        versial questions (political/
        social issues)   4 3 2 1
      more reading in French lit-
        erature   4 3 2 1
      reading of French magazines
        and newspapers   4 3 2 1
      more listening practice in
        class   4 3 2 1
      more listening practice in
        language lab   4 3 2 1
24) In which situation do you feel you learn
    the best? (Please circle one letter.)
      A. in a regular classroom with the entire
         class   yes   no
      B. in a group of 5 to 10 students yes no
      C. in a group of 2 to 3 students yes no
      D. alone
25) I would like:
      the opportunity to do a great
      deal more independent study
      in French   4 3 2 1
      the usual class meetings and
      regular assignments   4 3 2 1
26) Do you feel at ease when making
      use of the skills you are

learning in a foreign language?
```
   in listening                  4  3  2  1
   in speaking                   4  3  2  1
   in reading                    4  3  2  1
   in writing                    4  3  2  1
```
27) Some people tend to feel uneasy, or are afraid to make mistakes or to sound ridiculous when trying to speak a foreign language. Rate the extent to which you feel this way.   4 3 2 1

28) In these situations, who do you feel is most responsible for your uneasiness? Circle one letter that applies to you.
```
   A. yourself                  yes    no
   B. the teacher               yes    no
   C. the other students        yes    no
```

Comments:

SECTION IV:

ACTION

REPORTS

15. KEEPING THE DOOR TO THE FUTURE OPEN THROUGH IMAGINATIVE COURSE DEVELOPMENT

HENRY M. CORDES
College of San Mateo, California

Those educators who are sensitive to the
changing demands in the second language
field at the community college level may be
interested in some of the new programs we
have implemented at the College of San Mateo.
Our institution is celebrating its fiftieth
anniversary this year. We look to the past
with considerable pride and to the future
with reasonable enthusiasm. Our foreign language faculty includes eight full-time day
instructors and eight part-time evening
instructors.

For many years our foreign language programs in French, German, Russian, and
Spanish were geared to meet the needs of the
students who transferred to the nearby state
colleges and universities. The recent
changes in the language requirements at the

receiving institutions caused an expected drop in enrollments at our College, because many students, if not the majority, saw themselves as transfer students, even though that self-perception proved to be statistically inaccurate. Non-transfer students were usually treated like transfer students, however different their reasons for taking a foreign language might have been. "Academic standards" were the overriding concern of the teachers. We needed some changes.

In an article on pluralism in the community college, Altman points out that "efforts must be made to provide options for *all* students to attain goals in foreign language study of *personal value* to them."[1] Recent developments in individualizing instruction in the secondary schools point the way toward enriching the curriculum with courses that are meaningful to the full range of people who are served by the "open door" policy of the community college.

One of our first attempts to meet changing demands for language instruction arose from our knowledge that the local Berlitz and Sullivan language courses were drawing large and eager audiences willing to pay money to learn a language while our enrollments were dropping. A very enterprising French teacher on our faculty, Mrs. Rose Marie Beuttler, created our first mini-course for evening college students in our Community Services series, calling it *Survival French*. This mini-course meets five weeks for only two hours a week. It was designed to give the prospective traveler basic patterns to use for a few selected topics. We did not promise to teach anyone French thoroughly, but we did

give them what they wanted--some pronunciation practice and phrases pertinent to
travel. Our first class was a tremendous
success. Over forty-five people appeared on
the first night. We have added German and
Spanish to the list of these mini-courses.
They are now being presented each semester
to enthusiastic classes. I can also state
with pleasure that our beginning level
semester-long conversation courses in these
languages in the evening have shown greater
enrollments this year than last and will, we
hope, continue to grow and expand next year.

     Along with our traditional credit trans-
fer-level courses in the day school we decided this past semester to introduce a
beginning level conversation course in the
day program for two units of non-transfer
credit. These courses resemble our evening
school beginning courses. We had a conversation course in the day curriculum already, but it required at least two semesters
of prior study before the students were
eligible. We decided to take a chance on a
course for beginners only, hoping that those
who had interests in travel might register.
Of course we were somewhat afraid that we
would draw some students away from our regular first semester traditional course. Our
courage was rewarded with a pleasant surprise.
Our regular courses were not depleted and we
added a full class of French, German, and
Spanish elementary conversation to the day
curriculum. We came upon a new and different audience. Many participants were
housewives and retired people in the community. There was a healthy admixture of
younger students from the regular Day College program--those who did not want our
traditional first semester course. The

mixture of older and younger people is desirable and healthy in a community college.
These classes have pointed the way to the
future for us and we shall continue to offer
them. They keep interest in languages alive.

We now have requests for beginning
courses of this type for specific vocational
purposes. We shall have Spanish for Police
Officers as well as Spanish for Nurses. We
shall offer German for travelers and business people. We shall have French for air-
line personnel. We have already given a
course in Spanish for Social Workers and
will double the number of these classes in
the Fall.

We have learned that there is indeed an
audience for languages. There is a real
demand, but this demand requires a type of
instruction that is not always the same as
that which is given in traditional courses.
If community colleges can adapt to this
realistically we can extricate ourselves
from our presumed predicament.

The mini-courses and the beginning level
conversation courses have pointed the way to
the future for us. It is rewarding to know
that a percentage of people in these special
courses have later chosen to enroll in a
traditional course because they felt the
need for further language study.

We have learned to plan together. We
have stopped blaming the administration, or
the lack of a university requirement, or
other forces for low enrollments. We are
planning for foreign language courses with a
view to individualizing them wherever possible so that we may retain as many learners

as we can.

We shall experiment next with a reading track for special students. We are planning a topical survey of foreign literature in translation. We have already attempted courses for native speakers only, such as our Spanish 3n, so that we can give the native the special training he needs. We have also tried a half-speed traditional first semester course so that students who are fearful of language study or who have not been successful in the past may get a new start.

We recognize the problems in language teaching at the present time, and we shall continue to plan, to experiment and to draw renewed inspiration from those courses which have proved successful. We plan to keep the door to the future open!

NOTES

1. Altman, Howard B., "Foreign Language Instruction in the Community College: A Mandate for Pluralism" in Section I of this book.

16. DEVELOPMENT OF A CONVERSATIONAL FRENCH COURSE

ELISABETH WACHS
Parkland College
Champaign, Illinois

I had originally planned my conversational French course for only one quarter. It was to include simple conversation, basic vocabulary, and a minimum of grammar. Because the course was aimed at those desiring to travel in French-speaking countries, each session was devoted to a conversational topic of practical use for everyday life in such countries. Topics included how to handle transportation, count foreign currency, order meals, shop, and obtain lodging.

After the first quarter most of the students showed strong interest in continuing the course, for, as they progressed, they realized what potential opportunity they had for further development of their skills. I then devised a second quarter for the course in which I attempted to fulfill the needs and wishes as both the students and I perceived them.

I have just completed this second quarter and am working now on planning a third.

At the beginning of the second quarter I introduced the past tense (*passé composé*). We have been practicing that tense during the whole quarter and by now the students are able to answer rather spontaneously to a given question using the *passé composé*. Our main conversation still deals with everyday topics like: *Où avez-vous mangé ce soir?*
À quelle heure êtes-vous parti?
Êtes-vous allé au cinéma samedi dernier?

Unfortunately most of the students have very little time to work on the language at home, so the classwork consists mainly of practice. The students especially requested more practice in generating responses themselves in French. Accordingly we now spend the first part of the weekly class in practicing everyday conversation, using new verbs and new vocabulary. Each session I distribute a short reading text. This text consists of a story in a light humorous vein, usually containing a punch line or a riddle to be solved. I also use the stories to provide the opportunity for questions and answers in French on the content. Practice in pronunciation is a further benefit from this approach, which I prefer to regular drills.

The course is intended to put only a minimum emphasis upon grammar. Specific grammatical points are discussed on separate worksheets, which provide exercises as well.

This is usually done in conjunction with the reading in which the particular point of grammar is to be found. I ask students to study these worksheets thoroughly at home.

In addition, I prepare a tape each week containing the reading text plus the worksheet. Students may take these tapes home for further listening practice.

Occasional diversions from this pattern are provided by spontaneous discussions of current events, allowing the students to apply what skill they have in speaking French to a more practical situation. I have also xeroxed short articles and cartoons from *Paris-Match* for them to read and describe.

My plans for a third quarter of this course are not yet definitely formulated. I have asked for student suggestions in this direction, and have received some response. I shall take whatever student suggestions and requests I finally receive and put them together with my own ideas of what the students can accomplish in order to devise an outline for this quarter. At this point I envision coverage of the future tense, subordinate clauses, and whatever other grammar seems appropriate. Naturally I expect progress in more difficult reading selections and informal oral conversation.

The course is intended only to cover the speaking and reading of French. I have given no attention to writing skills.

17. A CONVERSATION COURSE FOR TERMINAL STUDENTS IN THEIR FOURTH SEMESTER

GLENDA J. BROWN
University of Northern Colorado

There are countless ways to stimulate oral
proficiency in a foreign language; our beginning classes have been directed toward
the so-called "oral approach" for several
years now. But how can one most effectively
make the transition from model sentences and
pattern drills to the two-way street which
is the essence of oral cummunication? The
following ideas arise from several experiences with conversation classes, dealing
both with students in a FL major program,
and more recently with those completing a
four-semester language requirement at the
University of Illinois. The methods developed for the latter group must necessarily
differ from those which might succeed with
a group motivated by a desire to excel in
their chosen major. Various levels of oral
proficiency within the group, fear, lack of
interest, possibly a pass-fail grading system,
all these and more are obstacles which must

be overcome if the language student is to
leave the classroom with the culture of another people.

"Having an encounter" is indeed an expression which describes one possibility of a
workable class atmosphere. It has been said
that effective oral exchange in the classroom necessarily involves playacting. Because the classroom situation is an artifi-
cal one, students must be made to accept the
this artificiality, and to throw themselves
into various situations proposed by the
teacher. The situations, however, must be
carefully selected. It is well and good to
announce that friendship with a Frenchman
will sooner or later entail an animated discussion of politics, and that you are therefore going to discuss politics in class, but
to bring the student to the point of being
able to function in such a situation, both
in terms of subject matter and animation, is
a task which cannot be accomplished in the
first or second week of class.

I have thus found it helpful to direct
the first few weeks toward a narrower range
of topics, still bearing in mind that a situation must be simulated so that the class
period will not deteriorate into a teacher-
dominated conversation. To "train" the
student for future discussions of a more intellectually satisfying nature, practical
situations can be created which increase ease
with conversational patterns as well as build
practical vocabulary. Travel information is
usually accepted as a source of useful vocabulary: airports, train stations, hotels,
hitchhiking, all provide a wealth of material interesting to the student. The ways of
conducting these interchanges are again many
and varied. A scene in an airport or train
station between traveler and employee or be-

tween friends preparing for a trip puts into
use vocabulary which has already been provided. If the basis of the situation is rather
a reading about hitchhiking, for example,
the situation simulated might be a dramatized
version of what was read, or a common endeavor between "journalists" who wish to compose a manual for hitchhikers. In both
cases, the humor and conventional expressions
probably present in the text should be easily accessible to the student and transferred
into his discussion or simulation. An even
better source of these conventional responses,
and of everyday vocabulary too, can be found
in taped dialogues, since they are already in
the oral form. Retention is of course more
difficult here; one possiblity for building
such retention will be touched upon at the
end of this paper. However, it is amazing
how students pick up even the style and in-
tonation proper to a tape series and transfer this into their oral presentation. To
cite an example: after exposure to a tape
series which consists of radio interviews, I
recently asked students to conduct interviews
with each other on a subject which had been
part of their reading material. The quality
of the resulting conversations was consistently good, among the weaker as well as the
strong students. Not only was the vocabulary internalized, but the exchanges were
lively and emotional, as were the taped interviews to which they had been listening.

By this point in the course the teacher
should have sifted out the various individual
problems plaguing the students, and have
helped them to correct these problems so that
the class might arrive at a somewhat uniform
level of facility by the middle of the semester. Here then is the time to broaden the
range of discussions topics; indeed, to begin the actual process of discussing in

earnest. The transition from "performing"
within a given situation to expressing one's
own thoughts about a topic of interest is
perhaps one of the most difficult ones in the
teaching of conversation. The student must
be helped to retain the facility he has gained during the first weeks of the course. He
must somehow be encouraged not to slip back
into the process of thinking of what he wishes to say first in English, and then trans-
lating it into the target language, uttering
an appropriate number of "uhs" and "ahs" to
allow himself time to perform this feat. The
subjects should be prepared carefully by the
instructor before they are given as material
for free discussion. If the topic is to be
politics, vocabulary should be provided in
such a way that the student will not have to
destroy his train of thought by groping for
words during the actual discussion. Sometimes this can be done simply by supplying
a list of expressions most likely to occur
in a discussion of this nature. Other times
it may be desirable to expose the class be-
forehand to an article on the subject, point-
ing out in class the different expressions
which they may wish to use. A transcription
of an interview may be especially helpful at
this point, as the style would already be
conversational. Once into the heat of the
discussion, the student should be able to
fall back on his previous practice with conversational patterns and his more recent as-
quisition of vocabulary, concentrating his
most immediate attention on the interaction
he must sustain.

The mention of interaction brings me to
a final point. As was mentioned at the beginning of this paper, the goal of the conversation class must be the two-way street of
real communication. And communication is
just that: a combination of speaking and re-

acting to the speech of others. Comprehension is, therefore, as essential as is the building of reliable conversational patterns.

It would seem, then, that part of a conversation course should be directed toward the acquisition of a more sophisticated level of comprehension. The best way to accomplish this is probably through a tape series, and there are many available, some complete with booklets containing summaries, vocabulary, questions and the like. However, I have recently become convinced that a taped dialogue or interview is just so much raw material which must be molded by the teacher into material suitable for his or her particular situation. It is with this in mind that I have just attempted the editing of a series of taped interviews, preparing recorded tape tests for each one. Bearing in mind the process through which a student learning a language goes as he is able first to distinguish, then recognize, then retain short utterances, I have divided the interviews into an appropriate number of parts, and dubbed in questions and true-false or multiple choice options. The student at first sees the answers, then only hears them, until the final step of writing out in the target language short answers to questions based on what he has heard is reached. The rewarding aspect of this project is the vast improvement made by the students and their apparent enthusiasm for the challenge presented them. When a group of students listens to a tape series on the laboratory telephone line (available from the University of Illinois Language Laboratory) almost twice as often each week as do students for other tape programs in the system, when after completing the tape test, the students beg to know the correct answers, one can perhaps with reason feel that some learning is going on, and interest

is being stimulated which will hopefully encourage these "terminal" students to continue their exploration of a foreign culture.

18. CAREER SPANISH

TOBY TAMARKIN
Manchester Community College
Manchester, Connecticut

Career Spanish, being taught this year at
Manchester Community College was designed to
fill a basic need in the two-year language
sequence. The need was felt for a more
practical approach to language study for
those students who plan to enter a career
field where the knowledge of Spanish would
enable them to carry out their tasks more
effectively. Many of our students are in a
two-year terminal program and plan to work
in the medical, social service, or retail and
business outlets in our immediate area.
Their employment opportunities will increase
if they are able to communicate effectively
in Spanish.

The program called Career Spanish makes
up the third and fourth semester of the language sequence. All students begin with our

101 course. They may then go on to either
102 (a traditional second semester) or they
may take 110 (Preparation for Career Spanish)
which stresses conversation and places
emphasis on those aspects of grammar which
are fundamental to communication (present,
imperfect, and preterite tenses as well as
commands and simple future tense; all pro-
nouns--especially direct and indirect
objects) and essential vocabulary. The
A-LM film series is used to "force" conversation, as recommended by Mills Edgerton in
the 1969 Northeast Conference Report, and
grammar points are extracted from the textbook as required. I also give them worksheets on the grammar to be mastered.

In the Career Spanish course, the student will work with 12 to 15 units which
deal with his future profession. These
units contain: a television dialogue filmed
on location using native speakers; audio
tapes with repetition practice; grammatical
exercises and patient or client questions to
be answered; a student lesson which does *not*
contain the dialogue but does have a vocabulary list, grammatical exercises, and the
same questions that appear on the audio tape;
and dittoed job-related forms to be used by
the student as he simulates his future work
situation. I also have transparencies of
all these forms as well as of the dialogues
for use on the overhead projector.

There are 25 units in all, containing the
following lessons (which were decided upon
after careful research to determine which
job situations were the most critical and
typical in dealing with Spanish-speaking
citizens):

MEDICAL	Two Emergency Situations
	Hospital Admissions
	Visiting Nurse
	Blood Test
	X-Ray
	Occupational Therapy
	Prenatal Care
	Dental Visit
SOCIAL SERVICES	Welfare Application
	Food Stamps
	Two Employment Situations
BUSINESS	Three Tax Situations
	Two Legal Situations
	Charge Accounts
	Food Shopping

These lessons are often double and deal with necessary job procedures and dialogues. The students and I go through the television dialogue, watching first. Then using the transparency I move from simple answers to questions and then to more complex answers. For the first lesson we go through the television tape (three to four minutes in length) at least four times. The third time we work with the transparency of the dialogue and ask questions which demand personal reactions or require recall of the students' personal experiences. Each unit takes two to three weeks to complete. When the student feels he has mastered the unit, he takes an oral test with me or with one of my many Spanish-speaking friends whom I invite to class to help me with testing and to add flavor and another accent to the routine.

The student is motivated because his experiences in the classroom are very much

as they will be when he is on the job. He
feels little pressure because he can wait to
take the quiz until he is certain he is
ready. He works in small groups and often
in pairs and has the joyous feeling of
communication in a new language by the end
of the first unit. The quizzes are often
complicated and take 20 to 30 minutes, as
with the unit on Welfare Application where
the student must complete with the client
all forms and, after extracting the information, decide what assistance the client is
entitled to receive; then he must explain to
the client exactly what he will be getting
(i.e., Food Coupons, Title 5, Title 19,
etc.) and make an appointment to follow-up
the use of these programs by the client.
The student must take all the initiative
from the first greeting until he completes
the situation. By the time the student has
mastered four units he begins to have
confidence in his ability to communicate.

I have seventeen students in the program
this year. Many were very poor first-year
students who would have normally dropped the
language sequence. All my students are earn-
ing A or B and the class is the most enthusiastic, fun thing I have ever done in ten
years of teaching. In their own time the
students have organized dinners at Mexican,
Puerto Rican and Peruvian restaurants; they
frequently visit the Spanish-speaking shops
and even watch the 11 p.m. television show
in Spanish recently begun here. They also
talked me into a Spring vacation together at
the Interamerican University in San Germán,
Puerto Rico. I have had numerous visitors to
the class and the members of the Spanish
Department at the University of Connecticut
were so pleased that they have granted full

transfer credit to the students taking our
Career Spanish course.

At present I am looking for a publisher
for these materials which took me almost
three years to perfect. I have had the
advantage of working as a social worker and
as a bilingual secretary, which helped when
I went out to research each unit. Publishers
I have approached are quite enthusiastic, but
since the program is very costly, due to the
dependence on audio-visual materials, I have
not yet received a firm commitment. I hope
to be able to report better possibilities
soon. I feel that the success of the program
lies in the use of either television or
motion picture dialogues and the special
method I use with these materials.

I strongly urge two-year colleges to
consider new approaches to language learning
so as to give students the continued incen-
tive they need to study languages.

19. SELF-PACED INTRODUCTORY FRENCH

MARJORIE A. BLANCO and MARY E. CHARRO
Prince George's Community College
Largo, Maryland

We, like many other foreign language
teachers, have been plagued by numerous
problems in the past few years. Our enrollment, particularly at the intermediate and
advanced levels, has dwindled each semester,
many of our students have very low motivation, and our very existence has been threat-
ened. Our students come from all socioeconomic levels and most of those who enroll
in our language programs plan to transfer to
a four-year institution. It was obvious to
us, at least three years ago, that our language program was falling far short of its
potential, and that something had to be done
to correct the situation.

During the summer of 1971, we developed
materials and learning aids for each lesson
at 101 level, and in September, 1972, our
self-paced program was implemented in three

sections of French 101. The program is built around Thomas H. Brown's *French: Listening, Speaking, Reading, Writing*, Revised Edition (McGraw-Hill). For every lesson the student receives a packet of written materials containing performance objectives, an assignment sheet (which tells the student how to proceed throughout each segment of the lesson), programmed grammar, videotapes with explanations of the structure contained within the lesson, and an audio conversation practice tape to supplement the tapes which accompany the text. The student must complete at least seven lessons to be eligible for a deferred grade which allows him to continue in the next semester; a student is given a letter grade for the course once he has completed eleven lessons and has taken a cumulative test over these lessons.

There is a great amount of freedom during class periods: the students can work individually, in small groups, or with the instructor; the instructor serves as a resource person and as a director of the learning process. A student chooses those types of learning activities which fit his cognitive style and proceeds through the material at his own rate. He must receive a passing grade on the end-of-the-lesson test before he is allowed to go on to the next lesson.

The program is structured in such a way that every student is required to do certain things for each lesson, e.g., written hand-in exercises, oral criterion test, dialogue presentation and end-of-the lesson quiz (testing both listening comprehension and writing skills). The program is individualized to the extent that it gives the student a variety of learning aids all geared towards mastery of the lesson. For example, some students just do not absorb written explanations, so the videotapes offer them an alternate means of learning the material; other students merely read the text, do the programmed grammar, and successfully master the lesson. Some spend hours working with the textbook tapes and conversation practice tapes to build oral ability and aural comprehension; others may simply listen once to parts of the tapes and be adequately prepared.

Currently all French 101 sections and three of the four 102 sections are self-paced; however, in September of 1972 the student will have a choice between a self-paced section and a traditionally organized one. This summer we plan to offer one 101 section and one 102 section in which only those students who are capable of handling the self-paced aspect of the course will be allowed to proceed at their own rate; the remaining students will follow a programmed course, but they will all be working on the same lesson at the same time.

We have not, as yet, made the program as individualized as it could be. It should not be necessary, in our opinion, for every student to master all four major skills in language learning to the extent that is now required. Many are interested in oral communication alone and do not need or want to write the language; others, especially those in science, simply want to be able to read French. This, to us, is the real meaning of individualization, but we continue to emphasize all four skills to insure that our students will receive full credit for their language study when they transfer to senior institutions.

Our classes range in size from fifteen to twenty students. We have no aides, and class time is often hectic for the teacher. However, we feel that the on-the-spot attention which *each* student receives is one of the most valuable aspects of this program. The teacher spends a great deal of time outside of class correcting hand-in exercises and oral criterion test tapes but does not have to prepare weekly quizzes or lesson plans.

It is too early for any meaningful evaluation of the program, but there are several comments which we can make. Some students are not able to assume the responsibility for doing the work themselves and need to be constantly prodded. More communication situations are needed where groups of students can put into use what they have learned; however, these are hard to provide when there may be only one student working on a particular lesson. Coordination of activities during the class period is sometimes difficult, because the teacher is needed for dialogue presentation, to answer questions, to set up tape portion of quizzes, and to diagnose problems and prescribe remedies. On the positive side, many students enjoy working at their own rate and not being forced to take tests if they are not prepared. Since students can re-take tests, the stigma of failure has been eliminated. They also feel that the wide variety of learning materials helps them to master a lesson with greater ease.

Although we know that there will be many changes in the course in the future, it is obvious now that many aspects of our self-paced, personalized French course provide positive motivation for students with a wide range of abilities and backgrounds. It is our hope that it will not only meet the needs of our students, but will also give them an enjoyable and profitable learning experience.

20. A SELECTIVE BIBLIOGRAPHY OF RECENT WRITINGS ON INDIVIDUALIZED FOREIGN LANGUAGE INSTRUCTION

HOWARD B. ALTMAN
University of Washington

A. Books

Altman, Howard B., ed. *Individualizing the Foreign Language Classroom: Perspectives for Teachers*. Rowley, Mass. Newbury House Publishers, 1972.

------ and Robert L. Politzer, eds. *Individualizing Foreign Language Instruction: Proceedings of the Stanford Conference*. Rowley, Mass.: Newbury House Publishers, 1971.

Gougher, Ronald L., ed. *Individualization of Instruction in Foreign Languages: A Practical Guide*. Philadelphia: Center for Curriculum Development, Inc., 1972.

Najam, Edward W., ed. *Language Learning: The Individual and the Process*. Publication Forty, Research Center in Anthropology, Folklore, and Linguistics, Indiana University, 1966. Also issued as *International Journal of American Linguistics* 32:1 (Part II), 1966.

Originally published as the Appendix to Howard B. Altman, ed., *Individualizing the Foreign Language Classroom: Perspectives for Teachers* (Rowley, Mass.: Newbury House Publishers, 1972), pp. 161-64. Reprinted with the permission of the editor and publisher.

Valette, Rebecca M. and Renée S. Disick. *Modern Language Performance Objectives and Individualization*. N.Y.: Harcourt, Brace & Jovanovich, Inc., 1972.

B. Articles

Altman, Howard B. "Individualized Foreign Language Instruction: What Does It Mean?" *Foreign Language Annals* 4:4 (1971), 421-22.

------. "Some Practical Aspects of Individualized Foreign Language Instruction" in George W. Wilkins, Jr., ed. *Dimension: Languages 71* Proceedings of the Seventh Southern Conference on Language Teaching, Atlanta, Ga. N.Y.: MLA-ACTFL Materials Center, 1971, pp. 13-25.

------. "Toward a Definition of Individualized Foreign Language Instruction" *American Foreign Language Teacher* 1:3 (1971), 12-13.

------. "Training the Foreign Language Teacher for Individualizing Instruction" *NALLD Journal* (forthcoming).

------ and Arnulfo G. Ramírez. "Beyond Micro-Teaching: Some First Steps in Individualizing Preservice Training for Foreign Language Teachers" *The Modern Language Journal* 55:5 (1971), 276-80.

Benardo, Leo. "Individual Differences in Foreign Language Learning in the Junior High School" in Marvin

Wasserman, ed. *Proceedings of the Thirty-Second Annual Foreign Language Conference at New York University*. N.Y.: New York University, 1966, 12-14.

Carroll, John B. "Individual Differences in Foreign Language Learning" in Marvin Wasserman, ed. *Proceedings of the Thirty-Second Annual Language Conference at New York University*. N.Y.: New York University, 1966, 3-11.

Bockman, John F. and Ronald L. Gougher, eds. "Individualization of Foreign Language Instruction in America" Occasional newsletter published at West Chester State College, Penn.

------, eds. "Individualized Instruction" Continuous column in *Foreign Language Annals*, 1971-

Gougher, Ronald L. "Individualization of Foreign Language Instruction: What Is Being Done?" in Dale L. Lange, ed. *Britannica Review of Foreign Language Education*, vol. III. Chicago: Encyclopaedia Britannica, Inc., 1971, 221-45.

Hanzeli, Victor E. and F. William D. Love. "From Individualized Instruction to Individualized Learning" *Foreign Language Annals* 5:3 (1972), 321-330.

Hugot, Francois, et al. "Innovative Trends in Foreign-Language Teaching" in James W. Dodge, ed. *Leadership*

for Continuing Development. Report
of Working Committee III, Northeast
Conference on the Teaching of Foreign
Languages, N.Y.: MLA-ACTFL Materials
Center, 1971, 90-141.

Jarvis, Gilbert A. "Individualized Learn-
ing--Where Can We Risk Compromise?"
The Modern Language Journal 55:6
(1971), 375-78.

Krill, Carole L. "A Confession: We Need
to Individualize" *Accent on ACTFL*
2:4 (1972), 6-8.

Logan, Gerald E. "A Comment on Including
Culture in an Individualized Foreign
Language Program" *Foreign Language
Annals* 5:1 (1971), 99-101.

------. "Curricula for Individualized
Instruction" in Dale L. Lange, ed.
*Britannica Review of Foreign Language
Education,* vol. II. Chicago: Ency-
clopaedia Britannica, 1970, 133-55.

Massey, D. "Individual Instruction: Its
Potential for Learning and Teaching
Modern Languages" *Canadian Modern
Language Review* 28:2 (1972), 21-28.

McLennan, Robert L. "A Guide to In-Service
Training of Teachers for Individualized Instruction in Foreign Languages"
Foreign Language Annals 5:2 (1971),
241-43.

------. "How Do We Allow FL Students to
Learn at Optimum Rates?" *American
Foreign Language Teacher* 1:3 (1971),
8-11.

Morrey, Robert A. "Individualization of Foreign Language Instruction through Differentiated Staffing" *The Modern Language Journal* (forthcoming).

Politzer, Robert L. "Toward Individualization in Foreign Language Teaching" *The Modern Language Journal* 55:4 (1971), 207-12. Reprinted in Howard B. Altman, ed. *Individualizing the Foreign Language Classroom: Perspectives for Teachers*. Rowley, Mass.: Newbury House Publishers, 1972.

Pope, Ernest. "Modified Individualized Foreign Language Learning at Gunn High School, Palo Alto, California" *Accent on ACTFL* 2:4 (1972), 9-11.

Reinert, Harry. "Practical Guide to Individualization" *The Modern Language Journal* 55:3 (1971), 156-63.

Shepherd, W. Everitt. "An Experiment in Individualized Advanced French" *Foreign Language Annals* 3:3 (1970), 394-99. Reprinted in Howard B. Altman, ed. *Individualizing the Foreign Language Classroom: Perspectives for Teachers*. Rowley, Mass.: Newbury House Publishers, 1972.

Strasheim, Lorraine A. "A Rationale for the Individualization and Personalization of Foreign Language Instruction" in Dale L. Lange, ed. *Britannica Review of Foreign Language Education*, vol. II. Chicago: Encyclopaedia Britannica, Inc., 1970, 15-34.

------. "Is Foreign Language Study
Relevant for American Students in
the 1970's?" in Sanford Newell, ed.
Dimension: Languages 70. Proceedings
of the Sixth Southern Conference on
Language Teaching, Jacksonville, Fla.
N.Y.: MLA-ACTFL Materials Center,
1970, 24-35. Reprinted in Howard B.
Altman, ed. *Individualizing the
Foreign Language Classroom: Per-
spectives for Teachers.* Rowley,
Mass.: Newbury House Publishers 1972.

Steiner, Florence. "Individualized
Instruction" *The Modern Language
Journal* 55:6 (1971), 361-74.

Sutton, Donna E. "Preplanning--An Essential Ingredient for Successful
Individualized Foreign Language
Programs" *Foreign Language Annals*
5:2 (1971), 243-44.

C. Related Works

Jakobovits, Leon A. *Foreign Language
Learning: A Psycholinguistic Analysis
of the Issues.* Rowley, Mass.: Newbury
House Publishers, 1970. (Chapter III:
"Compensatory Foreign Language
Instruction").

------. *The New Psycholinguistics and
Foreign Language Teaching.* Rowley,
Mass.: Newbury House Publishers,
forthcoming. (Part I: "The Language
Teacher is a Person Too" and Part II:
"Current Perspectives on Foreign Lan-
guage Teaching").

Kohl, Herbert R. *The Open Classroom: A Practical Guide to a New Way of Teaching*. N.Y.: Vintage Books, 1969.

Poirier, Gérard A. *Students as Partners in Team Learning*. Berkeley, Calif.: Center of Team Learning, 1970.

Rogers, Carl R. *Freedom to Learn*. Columbus, Ohio: Charles E. Merrill Publishing Co., 1969.

21. USE YOUR NATIVE SPEAKERS

DAVID T. COONEY
Polk Community College
Winterhaven, Florida

The employment of native speakers, under the work-study program, can be a definite asset to the development of an exciting and productive foreign language curriculum. The experience described below was initiated in our beginning Spanish courses which we have individualized. Native speakers, especially of Spanish, can be found among the local student population with a little effort. A ready source of personnel is also available within the foreign student population of most community colleges.

Students signing up for beginning Spanish receive an orientation on the first day of class. Grammar is taught with a completely individualized set of programmed materials available commercially. Students have reading and writing assignments and, during each class meeting, they have the opportunity of

meeting with the instructor, either individually or in small groups, to discuss any
problems they might have with the programmed
materials. The instructor is also available
at specified times outside of class to meet
with any interested students.

At the end of each unit students must
take a test. Tests are taken outside of
class and monitored in the learning center
of the college. The student must achieve at
least 80 per cent before he is allowed to
proceed to the next unit. Otherwise his
particular problems are diagnosed and he is
recycled through the unit. This approach to
the teaching of grammar seems to be quite
effective with the type of student found in
the average community college.

The main portion of class time is reserv-
ed for guided conversation. Students are
divided into small groups which vary from
day to day. The instructor and native language assistant encourage the groups to talk
and ask questions, based on some situation
in everyday life which has been introduced
to them. There are always students in the
class who are able to lead their groups
which are no larger than four. The native
language assistant will stay with a group as
long as it is having trouble getting started
or continuing. The emphasis is on role play-
ing and the students are encouraged to act
out their roles to the fullest extent possible. We cannot stress enough the value of
the native language assistant. The instructor alone is unable to keep five or six
groups going at the same time, and, if the
instructor is not a native speaker of the
language, the native language assistant is
even more valuable.

In our series, the first situation involves a tourist, on a street in Mexico, asking directions to a bank. After the students have found their way to the bank and to a few other places, we bring them into a restaurant for a meal and some entertainment, and then to a theater and a museum. During the course of the year, they attend a bull ' fight (which necessitates buying tickets), visit a school, make appointments to meet people and visit sick friends in the hospital, among other things. As a final course requirement, the students must create a story, told in the third person, and based on at least five of the situations in which he has found himself duing the term. He tells the story orally, of course, and must talk for three to five minutes. This effort is graded as either satisfactory or unsatisfactory.

A third part of the course requires the student to spend at least one hour each week in the language laboratory. The hour must be broken into at least two sessions. The laboratory is staffed with student assistants who are native speakers, which means that help is always available. All the commercial tapes are broken down into segments lasting no longer than ten minutes each. Students can then repeat any tape they choose or they can proceed to the next step. The tapes contain, for the most part, traditional audio-lingual structure drills.

During the orientation session at the beginning of the course, the students are told that they must complete a minimum of seven units satisfactorily to receive a grade of A. Six units will earn a B and five a C. Less than five units results in a grade of incomplete which is recorded simply as NG or

No Grade. The student then re-registers for the same course but begins where he left off. When he finishes the required work he moves on to the next level. Students who finish the course requirements before the term ends can continue with Level II. This means that a student can take as few or as many terms as necessary to complete the first two levels of elementary Spanish and not accept any grade other than A. This will earn him credit, on his transcript, for Spanish 101 and 102. We hope to be able to extend the program to the intermediate levels and expand it to include other languages.

The commitment which the college has made to the development of a systems education and to the individualization of instruction has required all departments to seek innovative ways to improve instruction. The approach, described above, will work only if it has the full commitment of the language staff and the administration.

22. CHANGES IN SEQUENCING OF CONTENT AT THE JUNIOR COLLEGE LEVEL

KARL S. POND
Miami-Dade Junior College South
Miami, Florida

The Foreign Languages Department of Miami-Dade Junior College South is characterized by two distinct feelings among its chairman and staff members. First, that there must be more than can be done to make the foreign language experience more valuable; and second, that new knowledge must constantly be sought and applied.

In view of these attitudes, the Department is attacking curricular problems on two separate fronts--the group learning situation on the one hand and individualized instruction on the other.

Goals for the two-year (4 trimester) package had been established long ago; the persistent problem, however, was that only a small percentage of students ever achieved

244

them. The majority of students simply never reached the simple communication goals and dropped out or turned off.

About a year ago it was decided that the learning of the entire fundamental grammar or basic structures, in two trimesters, was a totally unrealistic, artificial and unusually cruel goal. It kept all the instructors constantly busy ramming heavy, meaningless units of grammar down the throats of disgusted learners who had hoped to learn to use a language, but found themselves doing only grammar exercises.

The decision was made to combine the 101 and 102 courses into one six-credit course, meeting four or five times per week, depending upon the length of each period. The same was done for the 201 and 202 sequences. These changes allow for a more intensive, and perhaps even more important, for a more personal experience. The classes have a tendency to become a social entity providing greater opportunities for the development of personal relationships, a necessary condition if communication skills are to meaningfully develop in a class.

The most important decision, however, was to structure the content of the courses in such a way that the simultaneous implementation of the four M.L.A. goals could take place. The Department realized that it had always paid lip service to these goals, but that, due to the emphasis placed on the doctrine of "the sacredness of the whole grammar in the first two courses," the learner had been unable to learn to use his language skills.

Today, the "basics" are being spread over
the entire four trimesters. This enables us
more effectively to use reinforcing materials,
such as readings, conversational exercises,
audio-visual materials, and discussions.
The grammar unit now becomes a point of
departure for a meaningful experience in
language, rather than an end in itself.

No hard, foolproof data are available on
the results of these curriculum changes.
Personal observations, however, show a much
lower drop rate, more positive attitudes,
and a much higher percentage of students
continuing foreign language studies beyond
the so-called "required" four courses.

We are fully aware that these changes are
not new; the only thing new is that we are
finally carrying them out. The next frontal
attack is the development of diagnostic
instruments in basic phonology, morphology,
and syntax with short modular self-teaching
programs corresponding to each item on the
diagnostic instruments.

For example, in French after five weeks
each student must take a speaking test
involving 22 basic items of French phonology.
Each item is numbered. If the student is
unable to perform on any one item, he refers
to a reference sheet for the number of that
item. On the reference sheet he finds the
page and cassette references for phonetic
exercises dealing with his problem or problems. He may also avail himself of a free,
native tutor who has been trained to cope
with the problems and materials.

At a specified date the student must take
a second test at which time he has to

demonstrate that he can perform the items he had missed on the first diagnostic test.

Students are no longer told to improve their pronunciation or grammar as the case may be. Today their problems are identified and isolated, and remedial opportunities are given each and every student.

Outlined above are the two main attacks the Department of Foreign Languages at Miami-Dade Junior College South is mounting in order to win the hearts and minds of junior college students to foreign language studies. Other improvements are being carried out, such as peer-teaching and flexible scheduling, and more will continue to be made.

23. A NEW PROGRAM OF SUBSTITUTE AND SUPPLEMENTARY GERMAN LANGUAGE COURSES

JAMES McGLATHERY
University of Illinois

The German Department in Spring, 1972
initiated two new language-course sequences
on the second-, third-, and fourth-semester
levels ("102-104 levels") which may be taken
either as substitutes *or* as supplements to
the regular "four-skill" sequence, German
102-104. At present there remains no provision for choice or supplement on the first
semester or 101-level. Any one of the three
sequences leads directly toward fulfillment
of the Liberal Arts College's foreign language requirement. The student may even
chart his own course from among these
courses, since the College requirement
basically provides only that the student
complete a four-hour, fourth-semester level
course (or equivalent). For example, one
student who took German 101 last Fall is
currently taking *all three* four-hour,

second-semester courses. He presumably will skip to the fourth semester or beyond after this Spring.

One of the two new sequences (German 112, 113, 114) is devoted to *practice in speaking German*, the other (German 122, 123, 124) to *practice in reading*, with emphasis on non-fiction, especially expository prose. Both of these sequences are experimental in that vocabulary, grammar, syntax, and translation are not presented or drilled and are only touched upon tangentially in class. Instead, games and exercises which provide direct practice in talking and reading have been developed. The guiding thought in these experiments is to take quite literally the principles that we learn to do by doing and that practice makes perfect. No exercise is allowed which does not involve spontaneous speech in the speaking sequence, or thoughtful comprehension in the reading sequence. In these courses the object is to have the students constantly proving to themselves that they can say or read things in German, and that they are making progress in these language skills.

In the speaking courses the removal of the instructor from the center of attention is crucial. His role is much more that of a recreation director or athletic coach, since his task is to devise games which do not involve his own participation, yet accomplish his pedagogical purposes. The students most often correct one another's mistakes, so that the teacher largely relinquishes this function, too. Most of the exercises involve verbal "cueing" on the part of the class members. The students do not raise their hands and are seldom called upon; their participation is voluntary and spontaneous.

In a typical "talking" game, one student will begin a sentence and a second student will complete that sentence and start another, which in turn will be completed by someone else. No one, not even the teacher, knows just which sentences will be produced in this exercise. In another game, one student will call for a part of speech, e.g., "ein Verb", whereupon another student will oblige with, say, "trinken", whereupon the class will rapidly spout forth as many sentences with "trinken" as they can. When the flood of "trinken"-sentences subsides, a class member will call for another verb or other part of speech from his classmates. About once a week the class will form subgroups and carry on conversations, usually with the help of such visual aids as pictures, illustrated magazines, or even toys. On such occasions the students have a chance to make spontaneous use of phrases and clauses familiar from the more "structured" exercises or games. A balance of audio-lingual ("verbal model") and direct-method ("logical deduction") textbooks are used as sources for "language input", i.e., as grist for the (games-) mill, with the result that the students have a smaller passive vocabulary and a relatively large active vocabulary. There is little, if anything, the "speaking" students can understand in German which they cannot also spontaneously say.

The reading sequence, like the speaking sequences, depends for its effectiveness on appealing to the imagination and logical faculty of the individual student and of the class as a whole. If the "talking" games largely involve the students' giving and taking *cues*, the "comprehension" exercises are largely a matter of seeking and finding *clues* to the meaning and import of a passage. Similarly, if "one word leads to another" in the speaking courses, clues help the foreign language reader anticipate what comes next or what he may have missed. Students are encouraged to seize on a word, phrase or clause and begin to imagine what the subject of the passage is and how the argument or exposition is likely to progress. Meanwhile, he searches for further clues which may support or contradict his tentative idea of the passage's import. As the meaning of the passage gradually becomes clear to the members of the class, the teacher aids the students in recognizing complexities of grammar and syntax which are crucial for a correct understanding of the author's exposition.

Class days are equally divided in the reading courses (as in the speaking courses) between prepared assignments and unprepared classwork. The prepared assignments generally consist of a text and questions in English to be answered in English. The questions and answers constitute an outline of the major points made by the author in the text. On sight-reading days the student is not left on his own with a dictionary, but has the benefit of his classmates' contributions to the search for a clear understanding of a passage. All classes are conducted in English. None of the texts is edited, each comes from a book which represents a major contribution to the history of science, poetry, or philosophy, and each day the excerpt is from a different book. The student practices reading at *all* levels of difficulty *throughout* the sequence, but with emphasis on elementary and intermediate texts at the start and on advanced texts toward the fourth semester.

About half of our students follow the regular, "four-skills" sequence through the fourth-semester level. Another forty percent switch to the reading sequence after one, two or three semesters in the regular sequence. (These students almost always proceed to the next level *despite* the change of sequence.) About ten percent currently elect the speaking sequence, but this figure will probably increase over the next two years at the expense of the regular sequence. The result will probably be a ratio of 40% in "four skills," 20% in speaking, and 40% in reading.

Almost all of our students use the speaking and reading courses as substitutes, not as supplements, although there are some students who add a course from another sequence in order to gain additional practice in that skill. Normally such students take the supplementary course at the same level they have reached in their other sequence, but it is also beneficial in some cases for the student to drop back one, two, or even three semesters, if his achievement in that particular skill has been poor, which is more often the case for speaking than for reading. By designing our new sequences as supplements, not merely substitutes, we have been able to offer a program which provides both intensive and extensive work on the second-, third-, and fourth-semester levels, with the result that a student does not have to progress in lock-step fashion through four semesters, but can concentrate his work

in one or two semesters and then skip to the
advanced level and still have some choice
regarding the skills on which he will concentrate. We also offer an intensive course
in the regular sequence, which enables the
student to finish four semesters of "four-
skills" work in *three semesters*.

Our department also offers *one two-hour
supplementary course on each of the three
levels* beyond the first semester. A student
who has had one semester of German may take
a two-hour Introduction to German Studies
(German 142). After two semesters he can
take Practice in Conversation (German 153),
and after three semesters, Practice in
Writing (German 164). In the first-semester
course (German 101) there is a weekly lecture on German culture. Further opportunity
for study for language students on the
elementary and intermediate level is provided by topics offered under German 199,
The Undergraduate Open Seminar.

24. THE BEGINNING GERMAN PROGRAM: RETHINKING THE PROBLEMS

RICHARD C. FIGGE
University of Illinois

It seems an inevitable part of the straw man,
set up by opponents of foreign language requirements, that those of us involved in the
teaching of foreign languages fail to produce
fluent speakers of a foreign tongue within
four semesters. Since students who have ful-
filled the requirement do not exhibit near-
native proficiency, we are told, we have failed in an unrealistic undertaking and the requirement should be done away with entirely.

If in fact the early mastery of the four
skills of language were our only goal, we
would have to give in to this frequently re-
hearsed argument. But since in four semesters of German study it is not our chief
function to turn out fluent speakers of German, any more than four semesters of physics
are expected to turn out physicists, our
challenge is to offer a meaningful educational experience, not only to those students who

intend to continue with the study of language
and literature, but also to those students
whose foreign language career is limited to
the time in which they complete the college
requirement.

While our students are working on acquiring the four skills in their first year of
German, they are at the same time being exposed to the broader problems of language.
Our basic text for Beginning German, Lohnes
and Strothmann, *German, A Structural Approach*,
was selected partly for its excellent considerations of the workings of language. Grammatical rules are never presented in isolation from the logic of German syntax, and
since we are working with linguistic adults,
we are able to make use of their knowledge
of Englsih as a basis for comparison when
we discuss how German approaches such language problems as unreal conditions or tem-
poral relationships. The students' mastery
of German forms and structures is thus accompanied by a remarkable increase in perspective on the phenomenon of language.

During the first semester of German, one
class hour out of four per week is given
over to lectures by senior faculty members
on German culture, linguistics, and politics.
In this series, which varies somewhat in content from semester to semester, students are
introduced to the field of linguistics and
German's place among the languages of the
world. They are exposed to such diverse
topics as German geography, the culture of
city and country, German forests and viti-
culture, pagan Germanic elements in Christian
festivals, and problems of contemporary German foreign policy.

The conversation, reading, and drills of'
the classroom are supplemented by two ses-

sions of laboratory work per week. The first
of these sessions involves work with a series
of tapes of readings, dictations, and grammatical drills which accompany the classroom
texts. One of the most effective and useful
facilities of the Language Laboratory is the
telephone program which makes it possible
for the student to hear the current day's
tape by merely calling a university number.
There is in addition a "random access" number which students can call to hear any review tapes of their request. The second
weekly laboratory session is devoted to viewing the "Guten Tag" film series, produced by
the Bavarian Broadcasting Company in cooperation with the Goethe-Institut. The films
follow the careers of a number of foreigners
who are working and leaning German in contemporary Germany. This film series, which
is continued through the second semester, provides abundant material for classroom conversation and has been produced with a style,
imagination, and good humor which seem a minor miracle to those of us who were subjected
to the "educational" films of the forties
and fifties.

One further aspect of our program should
be discussed for the reason that it was introduced to prevent difficulties frequently
encountered in the inevitably difficult second year. Traditionally students have been
forced to ingest all of German grammar in a
year's time, in a manner reminiscent of
Strassburg geese, and then they have been
presented with literary texts and a dictionary as the reading phase of their career began. It is difficult to imagine this tedious
and strange new activity as a happy first
encounter with a foreign language. I exagger-
ate, of course, but what teacher has not been
aware of the difficulties inherent in the
transition from grammar to literature in inter-

256

mediate German studies?

   In our program we have sought to obviate
some of these difficulties by extending the
presentation of grammar into the third semester. The first immediate result of this
is that grammar is learned at a more leisurely pace, with adequate time for mastery
through practice. The more difficult aspects
of German grammar, such as the subjunctive,
time phrases, and aspects of word order, are
dealt with fairly early in order to give the
students ample time to work with them. Such
matters as the passive voice and extended
adjective constructions are treated in the
third semester, precisely because they present no great difficulties to the student
and consequently require little time for mastery. With the time thus gained in the first
semester we introduce the first of a series
of cultural readers. The readers are discussed in German in class, and *Nacherzahlung-
en* are assigned. We clear up any textual
difficulties the students may encounter, but
our purpose is to accustom our students to
reading more and more extensive material on
their own rather than to go over every sentence in class. The result is that by the
time we have finished our presentation of
grammar half way through the third semester,
the students are prepared for their heady
first encounter with modern German prose and
drama by Heinrich Böll, Luise Rinser, Sieg-
fried Lenz, Erich Kästner, and Wolfgang
Borchert. Best of all, since lengthy prose
reading assignments by this time hold no
terrors for our students, these encounters
are usually accompanied by the emotional responses one always hopes for in introducing
one's students to significant German literature.

25. DIVERSIFICATION OF THE ELEMENTARY AND INTERMEDIATE LANGUAGE COURSES

WILGA M. RIVERS
University of Illinois

Many people, many ways. We are continually reminded that our teaching should stimulate learning, and that learning is a highly individual matter: people learn through different senses, at different rates, and with different goals in mind. They are interested in different content. With over a thousand students in the first four semester courses[1] the French Department at the University of Illinois at Urbana has to provide some sixty classes taught by about forty instructors. Among these students there is obviously a great diversity of needs, interests, abilities, and learning styles. Among the forty instructors there is also a diversity of capabilities, special interests, and teaching styles. Most junior-community colleges do not have these great numbers of classes which permit many options;

258

nevertheless, a description of what we are trying to do at Urbana-Champaign may give junior-community college instructors some ideas for developing new patterns of instruction and content at this level.

The program as developed provides for differences in goals, pace, preferred modality of learning, and content. At the end of this article there is a summary diagram for reference.

GOALS

We recognize the fact that the great majority of students in our 101-104 sequence do not intend to major in French. (By far the greatest majority of our present majors and minors have already completed four years of high school French on entering the Liberal Arts College.)

We therefore provide for *continuing and terminal* students. After a common core of two semesters of language study, which enables students to decide whether they are particularly attracted to the advanced study of French, we provide a 133 and 134 *accelerated sequence for declared potential majors and minors* or others who wish to develop their knowledge of French at greater depth. These courses deamand a more intensive concentration on all four skills, treat grammar at greater depth, and introduce the student to the study of literature, while also providing a background in French civilization and culture. Classes are conducted in French and every effort is made to bridge the gap between the intermediate and advanced courses.

All other courses are designed to *provide terminal students with a satisfying experience of interest to them.*

Students who do not elect to take the continuing 133-134 sequence are not barred from advanced levels of French but are encouraged to do some further independent study in preparation for advanced level courses.

The terminal 103-104 sequence is then varied further in content and approach.

PACE

Students are able to determine their own rate of progress in various ways:

Placement tests are given to all entering freshmen with some high school French credits. These are used for diagnostic purposes to advise students of the appropriate level at which to continue their study of French.

Proficiency tests are given at regular intervals (second week of fall, spring, and summer semesters, end of spring semester) to enable students to move on a course if they have acquired sufficient knowledge.

Intensive courses meeting eight hours per week enable students to move ahead at a faster rate by combining 101 and 102 in French 105, combining 102 and 103 in French 106, and combining 103 and 104 in French 107.

An *individualized* 101-102 sequence enables students to work at their own pace for variable credit, taking two semesters, three

semesters, or one and a half semesters as
they require it to complete the two courses.
Students may transfer into this class from
the regular classes or out of it into the
regular classes if they need the individualized approach for a shorter period.

The opportunity to *retake tests*, or
parts of tests, to improve one's grade is
provided at all levels. Final examinations
have been eliminated at the 104 level, being
replaced by an overall grade for quizzes,
tests, individual projects, and class participation.

Independent study is available at the
104 level for students with special interests.

Language laboratory tapes are available
by telephone line, thus enabling students
to practice with taped programs as long as
they like, as often as they like, and at any
hour of the day or night.

MODALITY OR APPROACH

At the elementary level different classes enable students to study by an *audio-
lingual approach*, an *active modified direct
method* approach, or through *computer-assisted instruction with aural-oral practice* in
the classroom.

At the intermediate level, a 123-124
sequence provides a *reading approach* with
discussion in English for those who are not
interested in developing listening and speaking skills, while *Conversational French and
listening comprehension* are emphasized in

the 113-114 courses for students not particularly interested in reading and writing French.

CONTENT

In the elementary sequence the emphasis is on the acquisition of a core of language knowledge and aural-oral skills with some development of reading and writing skills.

French *civilization and culture* are introduced incidentally throughout the sequence, but at the 104 level students may elect to devote their time to the study of contemporary French life and institutions in 144, or to the differences in attitudes, values, and preoccupations in contemporary French and American society in 154. In the general 104 course and in the continuing 134 course, French civilization and culture are given equal attention with French literature.

French *literature* may be studied specifically in the course Readings in French Literature (124). The literature content of 104 and 134 varies and one assistant gave a 104 course in *Black Literature of French Expression* in the Spring of 1972.

Readings in the *General Sciences* are given exclusive attention in 164, with students being encouraged to select, with the help of the instructor, readings in the scientific area which is of particular interest to them.

In 174, students read French *newspapers and magazines* to which they subscribe through payment of a lab fee in lieu of a textbook.

Students with special motivation may
select *individual topics for independent
study*; they may be interested in French
business methods, experimental work in
microbiology, lives and work of French
painters, etc.

For a junior or community college other
possibilities for content in courses suggest
themselves and some of these are discussed
in other Action Reports in this volume.

A future development under consideration is the provision at 103 level of four
or five eight-week units with different
content (French drama, French advertising,
French film immediately suggest themselves),
of which students would select two to compose
their course in addition to regular language
study and practice.

INSTRUCTOR RESPONSIBILITY

Instructors in the 101-104 sequence have
a well developed training program consisting
of a graduate level credit course in the
College Teaching of Foreign Languages, a
demonstration class at 101 level, a class in
Teaching Techniques, supervisory evaluation
of teaching, and active involvement in textbook selection, course development, test
construction, and the handling of student
problems.

The developmental trend in our department is toward the establishment of small
teams, gathered around an experienced
instructor, working together in the elaboration of a particular course content or teaching approach. Such teams already exist in

experimental methodology, reading courses, computer-assisted instruction, and special intensive courses for architecture students preparing for study abroad.

SUMMARY OF PROGRAM

GOALS
Continuing
Terminal

PACE
Placement for appropriate level
General courses (101-104)
Accelerated groups (133, 134)
Intensive courses (105, 106, 107)
Individualized variable credit
  course (199)
Independent study
Proficiency tests for accelera-
  tion

MODALITY
Audiolingual
Active Modified Direct Method

(Approach)
Reading approach (123, 124)
Conversational approach (113,
  114)
Computer-assisted instruction,
  PLATO system

CONTENT
Literature (including Black lit-
  erature)
Civilization and Culture (144)
Contrastive French and American
  Culture (154)
Scientific material (164)
Newspapers and magazines (174)
Individually selected content
  (199)

NOTES

1. At the University of Illinois at Urbana-Champaign, 101 is the first semester course, 102 the second semester course, 103 the third semester course and 104 the fourth semester course. In our diversification we have retained the 1...3, 1...4 formula, numbering third semester courses 103, 113, 123..., and fourth semester courses 104, 114, 124... The College of Liberal Arts and Sciences requires the equivalent of two semesters of college level foreign language study for entrance credit and a further two semesters for graduation credit. This requirement may also be met by the equivalent of three semesters in each of two different languages. (One year of high school foreign language study is equated with one semester at the college level.)

26. FRENCH COOKING IN FRENCH: A NEW APPROACH TO FOREIGN LANGUAGE LEARNING

ANNE C. WRIGHT
Barrington High School
Barrington, Illinois

Last October, in a department meeting, the
foreign language teachers at Barrington High
School decided to try something new and different in course offerings for the 1972-73
school year. We considered many possibilities, mostly classes in civilization, history, and folklore. When a course in French
cooking, to be taught entirely in French, was
suggested, everyone agreed that it was a
good idea. Our department chairman was
interested but concerned as well. He fore-
saw many problems; he was worried about
scheduling, budget, and the reaction of the
Home Economics Department, whose cooperation
would be vital to the development of such a
course. Nevertheless, he recognized the
need for a new type of foreign language
course where students use the language in a
practical situation. He was eager to develop
a program in foreign languages which would

provide opportunities for the students to use the language skills they had developed in two or three years of traditional study.

Our primary goal for the new course is to further the students' knowledge of French by providing a situation where they can use the language in an informal atmosphere. Other objectives include the assimilation of a specialized vocabulary in a field which interests the student, and the learning of basic techniques of French cooking, and the cultural aspects of the cuisine which is such an important element in the French way of life.

The class meets for two two-hour labs and one single class period each week during the semester. The recipes to be used were chosen to give as much diversity as possible in the preparation of different types of dishes: hors d'oeuvres, fish, poultry, meat, vegetables, sauces, and desserts. We plan to complete one dish per week. Many of the recipes to be used can be made with several variations, such as *quiche au jambon, aux oignons, aux champignons;* or *soufflé au chocolat, au citron, au Grand Marnier.*

Because of the shared enthusiasm of the Foreign Language Department Chairman and the Home Economics Department Chairman, many of the problems that we had foreseen were overcome. Problems of scheduling, use of the Home Economics kitchens, and budgeting for new equipment were solved by the cooperation of the two departments.

Because of the high degree of student interest, which was much greater than we had anticipated, we are going to offer French

Cooking each semester. We hope soon to
expand our course offerings even further so
that the practical approach to foreign language learning will become an important part
of our curriculum.

27. THE ACTIVE CLASSROOM

BERNICE MELVIN
University of Illinois

For a foreign language teacher, especially one who is using the "oral approach," one of the major problems is *when* and *how* the student is to make the transition from mechanical response to free conversation. Many teachers feel that the first two semesters are best spent in pattern practice and directed dialogues. Meanwhile, the student who is rapidly losing interest is promised that these two semesters devoted to parrot-like activity will pay high dividends when, finally, by the third semester he will have internalized enough grammar and vocabulary to move from the mechanical to the spontaneous. Unfortunately, this move is seldom successful. Often, perhaps all too often, the teacher finds his first attempts to lead the students from grammatical drills to free conversation so painful and fruitless that he quickly abandons the task and, blaming

the failure on lack of preparation, seeks
refuge in more drills and workbook correction. The problem does not usually lie with
the student's preparation, or lack of it,
but rather with the gap between the time
when the student is first introduced to the
language and when he is given his first real
opportunity to "use" it. I have found,
while teaching beginning French courses at
the University of Illinois, that for all
students, prospective majors and minors included, the classroom experience is more
satisfying and useful when attempts to make
the student engage in free conversation
begin the first week. This is not to suggest that grammatical drill and directed
dialogue be abandoned but that they be
used as intended; as a means to an end and
not substituted for that end.

It is important that, from the very
beginning, the student have the opportunity
to use, in as many ways as possible, what
he is learning. As soon as the first
lesson can be improvised by the students,
much can be communicated with a few words
and some expressive gestures. As soon as
the students have learned the names of the
objects in the class they can play "I spy..";
or a student can describe an object which
the others try to name; or, as they learn
transitive verbs students can be asked to
pantomime a series of acts which the other
students attempt to describe.

"Play-acting" is a central part of a
language course that is conversation-oriented.
Beginning students get most of their practice
in speaking by acting out situations suggested by the content of a lesson. However,
role-playing cannot succeed unless the

teacher has the wholehearted co-operation of
the members of the class. Willing participation in dramatized situations is most
easily achieved in a student oriented class
directed by a teacher whose open, non-
authoritative attitude encourages a sense
of equality, self-respect and self-confi-
dence in the students. A small, but vital,
part of achieving the right atmosphere is
avoiding the tendency to undermine the student's confidence by over correction. A
student who is made to feel that *how* he says
something is more important than *what* he
says will soon give up trying to make novel
or personal statements and will, when called
upon, rely on programmed responses that risk
neither his ego nor his grade. Correction
is necessary but a student should never be
interrupted in mid-sentence or mid-thought.
When two or more students are talking
together I have found it best to make a note
of the errors for later correction, rather
than interrupt a conversation which, although not grammatically perfect, is being
enjoyed and understood by the class. Although the teacher could always provide a
word the student does not know or cannot
remember, the students should feel free to
ask each other, to draw pictures on the
board, or to act out that which cannot be
depicted--in short, they should use whatever means they have at their disposal to
communicate a thought or feeling to the
other members of the class. Students will
benefit more from class activities if they
develop the habit of listening to, correcting, helping, and questioning each other.
There will be little or no problem in getting
them to listen to each other if they are
regularly asked to repeat, to comment on, or
to correct what another student has just said.

The ability to understand what is said
is a necessary part of learning to converse,
therefore the teacher should take advantage
of every opportunity to give practice in and
test the student's listening skill. Present-
ing a new lesson orally, with the books
closed, helps to increase the student's
listening ability. New grammar can be
explained briefly, in English if necessary,
before starting the new lesson. New vocabulary (when written on the board and explained using drawings, pictures, or simple
definition) is quickly grasped. The text
should be covered twice: depending on the
format, the text can be gone through
verbatim or the content paraphrased. The
second time the text is covered I interrupt
the story or dialogue to ask the students
questions about the content, making these
questions personal whenever possible. After
the question and answer session the text is
gone over with the books open. If there are
any illustrations accompanying the lesson
these can be used in a variety of ways: a
student can be asked to describe the picture; he can be asked to ask other students
about the picture; or he can be asked questions about the objects in the picture.
Often it can form the basis of a cultural
discussion. For practice in both listening
and speaking, the teacher should tell the
students *short* stories (made-up by the
teacher or modified from ones he knows).
This is especially valuable if the language
laboratory is deteriorating or poorly supervised. The students are told to interrupt
the story at any moment to ask for clarifi-
cation of events or explanations of words
they have not understood. When the story is
finished they may be asked to write, in
English, a brief resume of what they have

heard. This allows the teacher to check quickly their level of comprehension. Another possibility is to invite a native, or near-native, speaker to come to class to be interviewed. The students ask the guest questions trying to discover as much as possible about his profession and background. Again, comprehension can be checked by requesting a brief resume. When there are no proficient speakers available, or when the supply has been exhausted, I have always found the students eager to interview each other.

After the grammar and vocabulary of the first lesson have been learned, the teacher should ask the students to act out carefully selected situations based on the text or suggested by the vocabulary. There are two possibilities: the students may be divided into groups of two or three and given five minutes or so to write dialogues which, at first, should be limited to three to five responses per student. The students then perform their skits for the class. The students who are listening to the performance may be asked to comment on the skit, to give a brief "plot outline," or to ask each other questions about what they have just heard. Also, the students can, and should, be asked to improvise dialogues based on situations suggested by the text. The situation to be acted out may be explained in English since very little conversing will result if the students do not understand the situation they are simulating. The impromptu dialogues can involve as many students as the situation requires.

Whenever possible make a change in the physical situation to avoid routine and

and limitation. If possible, take field
trips or bring in posters, magazines, and
assorted objects to class to turn it into a
restaurant, market, doctor's office, garage,
etc. If the desks are movable, rearrange
them differently to suggest new situations
(e.g., train, movie theater, dinner table,
etc.) It is possible in these instances to
have several different groups talking at
once, with the teacher going from group to
group as needed.

By the end of the first semester the
students should begin to give brief, individual talks. The talks should be prepared at
home and presented in class without notes.
For the first talks it is probably best if
each student brings to class an object that
he can talk about. Before a student begins
his talk, he must write any new vocabulary,
with explanations, on the blackboard. After
each "speech" the students may ask questions
or the subject of the talk can form the
basis of a class discussion.

When the aims of a class are not only to
teach the students how to read, write, listen
and recite but also to communicate in the
foreign language, the teacher must be willing to slow the pace and to spend more time
on each lesson. He must allow time for the
activities which permit the student to use
and internalize the new grammar and vocabulary before proceeding to a new lesson.
The slower pace which is necessary to achieve
the best results in a conversation-oriented
class should not be viewed as a lowering of
standards. On the contrary, the resultant
rise in interest, motivation, and enthusiasm
adequately compensate for the loss of speed
(the race is not always to the swift). As

one second semester student wrote, "I'm
breathless--not from racing through the text
at breakneck speed but from *talking*!"

28. ENGLISH AS A SECOND LANGUAGE: MEETING THE NEEDS OF THE FOREIGN STUDENT

DAVID T. COONEY
Polk Community College
Winter Haven, Florida

Many junior colleges have a small number of foreign students registered, but do not have the facilities to offer them an intensive program in English as a Second Language (ESL). There is another way in which these students can be served, enabling them to reap the benefits of their academic programs without committing the school to the expense of giving them special tutoring.

Most foreign students accepted at colleges in the United States are required to have a minimum proficiency in English. The importance of this requirement should not be overlooked. Without this minimum proficiency, the foreign student will most certainly fail; he should, therefore, be directed to an ESL institute before he is accepted into a junior college which has no special facilities.

However, even students who have been accepted frequently need extra help. Problem areas for them are the specialized vocabulary of particular courses, and their inability to read the textbook, comprehend lectures, take notes in class, and write tests.

With this in mind, we begin at Polk Community College by supplying each instructor with the names, native languages, and general English competency of the foreign students in his classes. He is asked to notify the foreign student advisor at the first sign of difficulty, whether or not he attributes this to a language problem. In this way we are alerted early enough to begin to attack the student's particular problem. Depending on how the problem is diagnosed, any one or more of the areas described below can be provided for. Help is given by one instructor assigned to teach ESL in cooperation with the academic instructor concerned. Each foreign student is required to sign up for this ESL course if it is felt that he has a deficiency in English. The foreign student advisor makes the decision based on all the information available to him. The course may be repeated as often as necessary.

Vocabulary. The academic instructor provides an active vocabulary list, which he considers basic, if the student is to pass his course. The ESL instructor programs for the student a systematic approach to aid him in learning this particular vocabulary. Taped materials are used and frequent checks are made of the student's ability to comprehend the vocabulary in context in both oral and written form. Because of the programmed approach, the student does most of the work on his own.

Reading. The academic or ESL instructor provides graded material covering the same general content as the student is studying in class, and a program in the reading laboratory is arranged to help the student increase his reading ability, both from the point of view of comprehension and level of difficulty. Again, much of the work is self-instructional, with the ESL instructor acting as a reading consultant.

Listening. The academic instructor is asked to prepare a tape (5 to 10 minutes in length) containing a short lecture in the content area being studied. As his time permits, he will continue to provide additional tapes, all of which can be stored for future use. The student listens to the tape as often as is necessary for comprehension. Sometimes the problem is simply one of becoming accustomed to the particular instructor's speech patterns. However, the student may be provided later with a written script, so that he can check his comprehension of the lecture material. In addition, other tapes or movies in the same content area can frequently be found in the media center, and these can be used to develop even further the student's listening comprehension.

Writing. The most difficult of all skills to teach, writing presents the greatest challenge. Students can begin with dictation exercises from material on the tapes provided by the academic instructor. Students are required to write short summaries of content material they have read, or to make outline notes from lectures given on tape or in writing. They must always rewrite any assignment which is considered unacceptable by the academic instructor. In this area, frequent contact is needed with the ESL instructor.

Testing. All of the above will be to no avail if the academic instructor cannot effectively evaluate the student. The academic instructor is asked to provide the ESL instructor with samples of tests, so that the student can become aware of the types of tests he will be taking. He is counseled in the way to approach both objective and subjective tests. His academic instructor is asked to look for content rather than mistakes in language when grading a test. In some cases the academic instructor will test the student orally, if the written test has proven to be inconclusive. Every effort should be made not to penalize the student for deficiencies in English, but to demand the same standard in content achievement as is demanded of all American students. This could also sometimes involve a retest.

It should be kept in mind that all foreign students will not experience difficulties in all of the above areas. The major task of the ESL instructor is one of gathering materials and diagnosing each student's particular problems. Much of the student activity can be self-instructional. For the best results, the ESL instructor should be working with a small number of students.

The methods described can also be used to prepare the foreign student for future courses in highly verbal subjects, such as

regular college English, humanities, and the
social sciences. We feel that when a foreign student is accepted with borderline
proficiency in English, he should not
attempt any of these courses during his
first term. When scheduling the foreign
student's program, care should be taken not
to place him in a class beyond his ability.
Even if his academic talents are sufficient,
a deficiency in English will cause him to
fail. Sometimes a 1/4 or 1/2 credit load
may be advisable in his first semester.

With careful diagnosis and provision for
improvement, all foreign students who are
accepted should be able to compete with
native students; and most of them will
acquire the capability in English necessary
to complete their programs successfully.

29. TESTING: A HURDLE OR A MEANS OF LEARNING

SAMIA SPENCER, Auburn University

PAULETTE PELC, University of Illinois

In the Fall of 1971, students in the elementary and intermediate French courses at the University of Illinois were given the option of retaking a parallel version of each test (or of some section of the test if they wished) a week to ten days later in order to improve their grade. We were interested in the students assimilating the material so as to be able to keep up with a cumulative program, not in merely finding out what they did not know. If they were willing to go back over the material to learn it more thoroughly, we were willing to give them credit for what they really knew. A careful tally was kept of results for the original tests and the retake tests at the 104 (fourth semester) level to see what kinds of differences could be observed.

The program for French 104 was drawn up

as a contract with students, issued to them at the beginning of the semester. The program in the contract eliminated the need for a final examination. A total of five cumulative tests at three-week intervals during the semester provided for a continuous review of the material. (The final grade for the course also included individual oral and written projects and class participation.) Each of the five tests consisted of three parts weighted as indicated below.

Aural Comprehension (AC):

One or more paragraphs in French were read by the instructor and students answered multiple-choice questions by selecting from answers printed on a sheet. Answers were right or wrong with no partial credit. 22 per cent

Grammar (G):

Various types of exercises, transformations, and completions. Partial credit possible. 33 per cent

Reading Comprehension (RC):

Short passages from the texts studied followed by multiple choice questions in French, and additional questions calling for comment on controversial aspects of the material discussed in class (to be answered in English). Partial credit possible. 45 per cent

The students had the option of retaking one, two, or all three parts of the test, with the assurance that only their best grades on either test would be counted.

Although 45.8 per cent of the students in the course were taking French 104 on a Pass/Fail basis, the response to the make-up opportunities was very favorable, the percentage retaking any test varying from 52 percent to 41 percent for the final test.

All students who retook tests showed improvement or remained at the same level except for five students out of a total of 391. The improvement was particularly marked at the E, D, and C levels. For some, this may indicate that they tried to get by with little effort on the first test and then were challenged by the system to work harder. For others it probably reflects the longer study time required to assimilate the material.

At first, students tended to retake only parts of the test, but as the semester advanced they retook entire tests, with the majority of those retaking the tests being concentrated in the lowest letter-grade levels.

The section in which most improvement was shown on the second attempt was grammar, with reading comprehension next, and then aural comprehension. This order probably reflects the greater number of single items for which credit or partial credit could be obtained in the grammar section and the possibility of obtaining partial credit for answers in the reading comprehension section, as opposed to the all-or-nothing possibility for the aural comprehension items. It also reflects the detailed learning required for the grammar items as opposed to the level of skill which is tested in the reading and aural comprehension sections.

The data also show a pattern of encouraging improvement at first, followed by a period of lessened improvement which culminates in a period of rising improvement as the semester draws to a close. Intuitively this seems to reflect the usual tempo of student study versus activities during a normal semester.

30. THE VOTE ON THE FOREIGN LANGUAGE REQUIREMENT AT THE UNIVERSITY OF ILLINOIS: STRATEGY NOTES

RICHARD T. SCANLAN
University of Illinois

At a meeting of the Liberal Arts and Sciences faculty of the University of Illinois in Champaign-Urbana on March 23, 1972 a vote was taken which reaffirmed the college FL requirement by a margin of about 2-1 (225-118). Strong support of FL study by the college faculty is probably due in the long run to the quality of the program and staff; however, a number of steps were taken by the FL departments to develop support for their case among the faculty. It might be helpful to others who may soon face such a vote at their own institutions to know about those actions which seemed most productive.

The FL departments were notified in December by the Dean that a standing committee of the college would introduce a motion at the March meeting of the faculty to terminate the FL requirement. (We have a graduation requirement of four semesters work in one FL or the equivalent.) A Study Committee was then appointed composed of one member from each of the major departments: French (Wilga Rivers), German (James W. Marchand), Latin (Richard T. Scanlan, Chairman), Russian (Frank Y. Gladney), and Spanish (Joseph H.D. Allen). A charge was given to the Committee by the heads of the FL departments to study the issues raised by the motion to terminate and to recommend suitable action both to the faculty as a whole and to the FL departments themselves.

Weekly meetings were held by the Study Committee during the next three months at which the following actions were taken.

1) The entire matter of the FL requirement was carefully studied and reports both pro and con were given. The following materials and sources which were used as part of our study were considered most helpful by the Committee:

A. A listing of FL entrance and graduation requirements by institution and various articles by Richard I. Brod analyzing these data were enormously helpful in allowing us to put our own requirements into national and regional perspective. These materials are available from: Association of Departments of Foreign Languages, 62 Fifth Avenue, New York, NY 10011.

B. *The Case for Foreign Language Study*, edited by James Dodge and available from the MLA-ACTFL Materials Center, 62 Fifth Avenue, New York, NY 10011.

C. *The Foreign Language Requirement in Colleges and Universities: A Bibliography with Abstracts*, compiled by Dolly D. Svobodny and available from the same source as B above.

D. *A Modern Case for German* by Maria P. Alter and available from AATG, 339 Walnut Street, Philadelphia, PA 19106. This book goes far beyond German in its attempt to develop a rationale for the study of FLs.

E. *The Demise of the Foreign Language Requirement--Cause or Symptom: An Enrollment Study*, available from Washington Foreign Language Program, University of Washington, Seattle, Washington

Various members of the faculty either volunteered or were asked to present alternate approaches (administrative, methodological, or in terms of course content) to the requirement. The Committee decided on the basis of the evidence to support the FL requirement as it currently existed.

2) All possible objections to the requirement were considered and an answer was prepared either for distribution to the faculty or for use on the floor at the meeting. Arguments to be used at the meeting itself were assigned to various members of the FL departments as their own responsibility to develop and present so that many different people would be speaking from an informed position. It was pleasing to see that no argument against the requirement arose during the entire meeting (eight hours in length, extending over an eight day

period) which had not been anticipated by the Study Committee.

3) The State Department of Public Instruction was notified of the crisis and a strong letter of support came from all of the FL supervisors in Illinois.

4) Members of the College Standing Committee who disagreed with the majority position to propose termination of the FL requirement were encouraged to prepare a minority report which attacked all of the basic arguments in the majority position. This document was circulated to all members of the faculty.

5) A special effort was made to explain the issues of the debate to reporters from local newspapers. As a result we obtained excellent coverage and the papers were consistently and strongly in support of the requirement.

6) An eight-page document prepared by the Committee and detailing reasons for support of FL study and for the requirement was distributed to the faculty as a whole.

7) Committee members thoroughly familiarized themselves with Robert's *Rules of Order* which is the procedural guide for faculty meetings.

8) A special meeting of the FL faculty was called to discuss the upcoming debate. The Study Committee presented the general strategy it would employ and answered questions which faculty members had about the issue.

9) Graduate students from the FL departments

were organized to distribute informational materials on FL study to undergraduate students. Many graduate students were also present as members of the gallery during each meeting of the faculty at which the question of the FL requirement was discussed. While they were not allowed to vote, they could at least express vocally their reaction to various points made.

10) Telephone messages and reminder notes about the meeting were sent to those faculty members who were *amici causae*.

11) One person friendly to the study of FLs in each department was asked to be in charge of bringing to the meeting those members who supported FL study.

12) In addition to the substantive remarks which the Committee had prepared for the meeting, a number of alternate procedural plans were ready to be used if the necessity arose.

While it is difficult to evaluate the significance in the final vote of the advance preparation by the Study Committee, there is no question in the mind of each of us who served on that Committee that the entire issue was faced more clearly, intelligently, and with greater organization than if there had been no local group studying the matter and organizing the faculty.

31. A FRENCH CAMP IN CENTRAL ILLINOIS: COOPERATION OVERCOMES THE COST FACTOR

PAUL GRIFFITH, University of Illinois

VIVIAN MASTERS, Illinois Central College, East Peoria, Illinois

There is no need to let fear of financial and logistical problems stand in the way of setting up a language camp, if the experience of a group of French teachers in central Illinois is any indication. These teachers found that their initial misgivings about being able to provide food, lodging, native speakers, and money for such a large undertaking quickly vanished when they joined forces on their French camp project. Moreover, the teachers were so pleased with the camp that they hope to repeat the experience soon and even increase the length of the program.

We are all aware that a language camp can give students an opportunity to speak informally in the language

with natives (perhaps for the first time)
and to exchange ideas with them. It provides occasion for exposure to the foreign
culture and for sampling the national cuisine. What is more, this enrichment goes on
in the pleasant setting of a camp, with its
games, songs, campfires, sports, and relax-
ing camaraderie. But the spectres of housing and feeding a large group, of recruiting the participants and the foreign personnel, of organizing and financing the undertaking, too often discourage teachers from
doing more than wistfully relisting the
advantages of a language camp.

The Illinois teachers found that a Boy
Scout camp near Peoria would rent its facilities to them for a surprisingly modest sum.
Furnished cabins, a large meeting shelter
and dining hall, a completely equipped
kitchen, and the services of the camp ranger
were put at the disposal of the group. As a
bonus especially for a French program, the
camp was located on the wooded highlands
overlooking the Des Plaines River, down
which Marquette and Joliet made their way in
the earliest explorations of this part of
New France.

The meals, all featuring French dishes,
were planned and prepared by one of the
teachers, seconded by a hired assistant.
The other teachers supervised the remaining
activities: the campfire, skits, films,
group singing, games, conversation sessions,
even dishwashing and table waiting. A cadre
of young native speakers was recruited among
the French and Canadian students attending
the University of Illinois. This enthusiastic team added to the program an air of

291

authenticity rivalled only by the cuisine,
as they lead the group singing, directed the
skits, conducted conversation sessions, and
taught French games to their new American
friends.

By settling for low-cost housing, by
adopting economical menus, and by relying
heavily on volunteer personnel -only the
assistant cook received a salary- these
teachers were able to provide an enriching
experience at a price many of their students
could easily afford. By involving a great
number of teachers and even some students in
the planning, tremendous interest came already built in, as well as yet another
saving: no money at all had to be spent on
publicity. The combination of low fees and
high enthusiasm made recruitment easy:
students were signing up and paying their
deposits several months before the program
began, and enrollments eventually had to be
closed to prevent overcrowding. While this
initial experiment was only one extended
weekend in length, the teachers are confident a week-long or even a two-week camp
would be just as popular.

The lessons that these Illinois teachers
learned are valuable to planners of language
camps anywhere. For one thing, housing need
present no difficulties. Scouts, 4-H Clubs,
WMCAs, and churches often have camps that
they would much rather rent out, once their
own camp season has ended, than leave vacant
and unproductive. If the camp has deluxe
facilities or an enviable setting, the rent
can be rather high. But it is not necessary
to go to the mountains or to the north woods
to speak French. These Midwest students

made do very well with a river bank in
Illinois. Also not to be overlooked are
facilities available in state and national
parks. Even the campuses of small liberal
arts colleges might offer the required
logistics and seclusion during spring break
or summer vacation. Naturally, using nearby campus also eliminates the cost in time
and money that would be involved in trans-
porting the group to some distant place.

Salary costs can be kept down by maintaining an atmosphere that invites volunteer
help. The Illinois teachers say the camp as
a superb opportunity for their students who
had never met a Frenchman or seen a French
film; and they gladly gave their services as
counselors so that their students could
participate. The teacher who took charge
of the kitchen, a sister who had frequently
cooked for the large religious community in
which she lived, was a gourmet chef at
heart; and she considered herself rewarded
quite enough just by having an appreciative
audience for her talents. The young French
monitors had all arrived only recently on
the University of Illinois campus and looked
upon the camp as an opportunity to build
some international good will and to make
friends quickly with people in the area.
Finally, from the students themselves, who
were called on to share in the cooperative
effort by serving the tables, sweeping the
dining hall, and washing the dishes, not one
complaint was heard. They seemed to think
one or two little work details per day were
a small enough price to pay for the experience and good time they were having.

Thus, aside from room, board, and
mileage for the teacher-counselors

and the French monitors, there was virtually
no expense for staff for the entire three-
day program. Naturally, if the camp is
extended to a week or two, it might become
appropriate to reimburse the program director, the cook, and the monitors at least
partially for their time and talents. But
if the emphasis can be kept on the fellow-
ship, good times, and experience to be had,
the teachers will very likely continue to
support the program without giving a thought
to collecting any pay. If some reward does
seem in order, rather than a token salary
(which is all such an undertaking could
afford), the teachers would probably prefer
that the money be spent to provide a high
quality professional workshop conducted by
state consultants, publishers' representatives, and experts from nearby universities,
who would hold their sessions while the students were engaged in activities with the
monitors. In this way, the camp would take
on yet another dimension that should attract
even more teachers and consequently their
students.

The regional office of the French
Cultural Services is an excellent source of
free films, posters, maps, and records for
such a camp. The French are particularly
generous in this respect; but the consulates of other countries are willing to
provide what help they can to teachers of
other languages. A visit to the consulate
or a letter explaining the camp should be
enough to secure a pledge of some assistance
and materials.

Food is the biggest expense in the budget,
so the kitchen must be supervised by someone
familiar with shopping and cooking for large

groups. The Illinois camp found it possible to serve authentic French dishes and still keep the grocery bill within reason. It presented no little challenge to create menus that were French but still (1) were within the budget, (2) could be prepared in large quantities, and (3) would appeal to the American teenagers and young adults present. They solved the problem by preparing specialties like *boeuf bourguignon*, *poulet bonne femme*, *pot-au-feu*, omelets, *croque-monsieurs*, and other dishes using the cheaper cuts of meat, poultry, and meat substitutes such as eggs and cheese. The cuisines of other countries present even less costly possibilities. The Continental breakfast, with its disdain of eggs, ham, bacon, fruit juice, and other costly commodities, should definitely be adopted, as it provides economy along with authenticity. Those Americans who find it difficult to get through the morning on such scant fare could perhaps be treated to a mid-morning apple or cup of hot chocolate.

The fees paid by the Illinois campers completely covered the cost of the program. By keeping their expenses down and their enrollment up, the organizers were able to offer a successful camp, without any outside funding whatever. But their success was due not to enthusiasm and wise budgeting alone. They began with a very carefully worked out program. And here a word of caution is in order:

As any seasoned camp staffer knows, it is not enough to bring together good food, eager campers, spirited song-leaders, clever drama coaches, skilled recreational directors, and a beautiful natural setting.

Without adequate guidance and without *esprit de corps*, the program will simply not come off. Nothing brings on a flagging spirit more quickly than lack of direction. A clear-cut and workable schedule must be established for each day, from the reveille hour to the precise time for lights out. If Jean-Pierre brings out his guitar after dinner and a songfest ensues, that is because he was cued to do so by a program set down in advance. It would be ideal if such things happened spontaneously, and sometimes they do; but we cannot count on it. As a precaution, something had better be planned for every moment. Too much unstructured time in a group situation leads to a feeling of disorientation and futility; and few things will undermine morale more quickly.

Let us emphasize that a *group* activity does not have to be organized for every hour in the day. Some time slots will be designated "free time," "conversation time," or "clean-up time"; but the fact remains that these activities should be planned as part of the well-balanced ensemble. Even the various activities themselves should be structured for maximum efficiency and appeal, so that if Marie-Thérèse rises at the campfire to lead "Alouette" right after the "Bretagne" cabin has presented its skit, it is not because she was the only one inspired to get up at that moment. And let us not forget to back up every outdoor activity with a rainy-day contingency project.

A certain amount of pre-program orientation will also help things get off to a good start and continue to run smoothly. Instructors in their classrooms could teach the songs, assign some writing of skits and some work with camp vocabulary. Several weeks before the Illinois camp got under way, the students all received a mimeographed booklet in French containing the schedules, the menus, biographies of the French and American staff members, a vocabulary list, a clothing list, and the words of the songs to be sung at the campfires and songfests.

The Illinois group first became interested in their project at a meeting of the AATF Chapter early in the spring of 1971, and the camp was held the following September. The Peoria-area AATF coordinator, Mrs. Penny Pucelik of Bradley University, became the camp director. The teachers working with her were Mr. Marwan Nahas of Carl Sandburg College in Galesburg, Mr. Tom Swegle of Sherrard High School, Mrs. Gail Hopkins of Farmington High School, and from Peoria, Sister Loretta Bernier of Bergan High School, Sister Carroll Cradock of the Academy of Our Lady, Mrs. Vivian Masters of Illinois Central College, and Mrs. Patricia Martin of Bradley University. It is quite significant that the planning and participation cut so thoroughly across school lines. High schools, junior colleges, colleges, and universities, public, private, and parochial schools alike, all worked toward a common goal. This illustrates very aptly that even with modest means and scant experience teachers can bring off some very worthwhile projects through cooperation.

32. STUDY AND TRAINING ABROAD FOR COMMUNITY COLLEGE STUDENTS

GABRIEL SAVIGNON
University of Illinois

Two-year community colleges in Illinois
ought to offer their students opportunities
to broaden their views and to acquaint themselves with cultures different from their
own. The existence of year-abroad programs
in a good many four-year colleges and universities bears witness to the realization that
an experience abroad benefits practically
every language, fine arts, and social science
major. Every year college and university
students leave by the thousands for summer-,
semester-, or year-long stays abroad. They
do so either under the aegis of their home
institutions, as participants in more or
less structured programs, or strike out on
their own after having been promised a
certain number of credits upon the completion
of satisfactory work at a school or university abroad. Thanks to the cooperation of
many people here and in host countries and

to the usually serious performance of American students abroad, these students return to their campuses as mature, confident, perceptive men and women. They are eager to push forward in their studies and to help attract newcomers to their fields of concentration.

By their very nature, programs abroad in senior colleges and universities attract mostly language students. Should the same be true as far as community college students are concerned? Not necessarily. Obviously some linguistic preparation should be a criterion of eligibility for spending time abroad, but the student needs not be a language major wishing to become a foreign language teacher, an interpreter or a diplomat. Community colleges are unique in their emphasis on professional or vocational instruction and training, preparing men and women for careers as mechanics, cooks, contractors, repairmen, fashion designers, farmers. It seems to me that students interested in any of these vocations, the list of which is not intended to be complete, could benefit greatly from instruction and training in a country famous for such pursuits. I cannot think of a more relevant thing to do than to enroll a future chef in a French *école hôtelière*, a prospective fashion designer in a *maison de haute-couture* in Paris, a watch repairman in a Swiss or French *école horlogère*. As a large exporter of farm and construction machinery and of farm and industrial products, Illinois owes it to itself to see that its export organizations are staffed with men and women not only competent in their own specialty but also familiar with the culture of the countries where the state's products are sold.

In its dealings abroad the Caterpillar Company, for example, must rely on a whole staff of promoters, sellers, assemblers, and repairmen who are well versed in the language and the mores of countries where Caterpillar products are sold and serviced.

The foreign trade balance between Illinois and the rest of the world is certainly in favor of our state, yet enough Japanese, German, Swedish, Italian, and French cars are sold in the larger cities to warrant satisfactory servicing of the foreign automobiles. Young American mechanics, therefore, with an adequate command of technical French, Italian, Swedish, German, and Japanese could very well be trained in car plans abroad before starting their jobs in Illinois.

A study abroad program in some African countries where English is widely spoken would enable community college students to contribute their particular skills in a mutual exchange of benefits, while learning to appreciate the way of life of a different people. Latin America and the Caribbean should not be forgotten as other important regions for consideration. I believe these specific examples are sufficient to convey my point on the necessity of some kind of study and training programs abroad for Illinois junior-community colleges as an integral part of their vocational emphasis.

Community colleges also serve the four-year institutions of higher learning of Illinois in that a certain percentage of students transfer to senior colleges and universities. Those students who aim at fields in which a knowledge of a foreign

language and culture is desirable and who
will have had some study and/or training
experience abroad will be able to perform
very well indeed. Because of the duality of
function, i.e., a vocational as well as
liberal arts tradition, community colleges
ought to provide their students with time
and curricula for study and training abroad.

We will now turn our attention to how
such an experience abroad can be formulated
and implemented.

First, it seems desirable to strive for
a high degree of cooperation and coordination among the junior college districts on
the matters of planning, establishing, and
implementing study abroad programs. Cost,
the need for assurance of good standards and
the desirability of a cross-fertilization of
ideas are among the main factors that point
to the creation of some sort of a centrally
located clearing house.

Due to the availability of no more than
two years of schooling in the colleges, it
would probably be unreasonable to establish
stays abroad in excess of one semester in
length. The four months corresponding to
the first or second semester of the second
year seems to be a suitable time for a community college student to be abroad. Most
of the summer preceding or following the
semester abroad could also be used as an
integral part of the experience, fulfilling,
for example, the orientation and instruction
part of the stay in the case of the summer
preceding, and the training or in-service
aspect in the case of the summer following.
Either combination would give community college students approximately six months of

residence in a foreign country.

The countries to receive community college students can easily be identified on the basis of professional, educational and/or personal interests. Locations of schooling and training within each foreign country must be selected, however, not only according to student interests, but also, and above all, on the merit of the facilities offered: professional and technical schools, secondary schools, university centers, and/or industries. A set-up could also be arranged whereby a student spends part of his study abroad in one location and then moves to another for the practical aspect of his residence abroad, a sort of on-the-job training or work experience.

A good many university centers of Europe have become so saturated with students from abroad that it seems advisable to turn to other locations where community college students would not find themselves in the midst of whole colonies of fellow countrymen. In order to prevent a similar situation this time created by the temporary migration of community college students abroad, it would be well to think in terms of only 12 to 15 students in the same location at one time. Such a small number of students in one place would no doubt necessitate the staking of several locations within one country and require a substantial effort of coordination and, at times, of supervision. This effort could be shared, however, by a local coordinator and by a couple of roving representatives from the Illinois community college system.

I have already touched upon the necessity

of establishing two phases within the stay
abroad of every community college student:
a first phase consisting of a period of
schooling at a foreign vocational institution, university or secondary school,
according to the students' interests and
future plans, and a second phase made up of
a training session or work experience which
would enable the student to practice abroad
what he really needs for his future career
or for self-satisfaction or fulfillment.
I deem this second aspect of the stay of an
American student abroad very important for
chiefly three reasons. First, it is a
healthy counterpart to the typical classroom situation where a certain amount of
artificiality prevails and where the relationship between teachers and students
remains all too often a one-way affair.
Secondly, the implementing of acquired
knowledge through actual situations and
actions better prepares for every-day career
needs. Finally, but importantly, a period
of practical training enables every student
abroad to participate fully in the life and
culture of a people through the varied and
rich contacts resulting from finally doing
what the student likes to do, even on a
small scale.

In order to insure the success of the
study and in-training aspects of a program
abroad, the personal well-being of the students involved must not be overlooked.
Through a certain amount of cultural orientation involving readings, talks, discussions,
observation, and a guided initial experience
in the foreign country, students will find
the differences of cultures and ways of life
less a shock. This orientation should be
provided both before leaving the U.S. and on

the spot in the host country, preferably
with the help of persons familiar with both
countries and cultures. Such orientation
sessions for a whole group of students
going to the same country can be advanta-
geously carried out in one location, both in
Illinois and in the country of destination.
After the dozen or so students have settled
in the particular town of their residence
abroad, informal periodical meetings might
be planned in order to insure a smooth
acculturation in the host country.

Housing arrangements are of such importance as to leave with the students a lasting impression of their stay abroad. The
small size of a community college group in
one location makes it possible and advisable
for each young American to be housed with a
family and to participate as fully as possible in their way of life. Meals and activities shared with the family contribute
greatly to this participation. Recruiting
families ahead of time could be made an
additional responsibility of the two
American supervisors in residence in the
foreign country.

It is my feeling that through his contacts as a student trainee and temporary
family member the student should be able to
establish for himself a program of extra-
curricular activities. Travel and sightseeing are also made easy by the usual
vacations for Christmas and Easter, as well
as over weekends.

The transportation of community college
students between the United States and foreign countries does not present any serious
problem, thanks to the existence of youth

air fares and charters, particularly across the Atlantic.

While I have attempted in these pages to outline the rationale and procedures for creating programs enabling community college students to study and to receive training abroad, I would feel remiss if I did not urge the faculty and administrators of Illinois community colleges to consider the corollary of the proposal. That is to say, at the same time that American men and women study abroad, let us make it known that foreign students will find the same kind of study and training opportunities in Illinois through the good offices and facilities of our community colleges.

The following organization is very helpful in the general planning of the curricular aspect of a study abroad program (it also specializes in air transportation [charters] for students): Council on International Educational Exchange, 777 United Nations Plaza, New York, NY 10017. For specifics on the educational system of a foreign country as well as for the names of school and university administrators, one should contact the Cultural Attaché and request the services of that country's embassy.

33. **DEVELOPING A SHORT-TERM OVERSEAS STUDY-TRAVEL PROGRAM: PRACTICAL CONSIDERATIONS**

PAUL T. GRIFFITH
University of Illinois

A foreign study and travel program of a
month or two would be appropriate for many
colleges whether a year abroad has been
established or not. The shorter, less expensive program would provide an overseas experience for students unable to afford either
the time or the money for the longer sojourn.
In schools where the year abroad has failed
to win approval, a successful program of
three to eight weeks may eventually open the
way for a semester-long and ultimately a
two-semester overseas session. Certainly,
the value of the short program cannot be
questioned, for on a day-for-day basis, its
limited duration allows an even more concentrated exposure to the foreign culture.

The program can take many forms: travel
with study, travel only but firmly built on
pre-departure study, a basically academic

program with weekend excursions and field trips. The group can travel during the summer or between semesters and for any length of time available. These are matters for each college to decide for itself.

Let it be observed that a program of solid study, however well-meaning, would be very disappointing to students who had come a great distance at considerable personal expense only to find themselves confined to classroom and library. They would be better off at home. And persons who would insist on a too strong dose of formal instruction are overlooking the face that associations with the local people and well-structured educational travel are learning situations at least as valuable as the activities going on in the classroom. Obviously, if instruction from native teachers were our only concern, the far easier and cheaper solution would be to bring the foreign teacher to the U.S. campus.

Travel, meeting the people, and soaking up local color are major justifications for such a program, and adequate time for these activities must be built into the schedule. At the other extreme, a trip that is all mere rubberneck sightseeing can scarcely be justified as a school activity and would be better left to student travel agencies. The best program, it seems, would combine all elements: a thorough orientation to provide cultural, historical, artistic, and linguistic background on the areas to be visited, followed by a tour structured as an extended field trip with as many classroom sessions or group discussions as needed to refresh the background and to reinforce appreciation of the places visited.

WINNING ADMINISTRATIVE APPROVAL

School administrators have a right to be concerned about the legal aspects of foreign travel, the academic worth of the program, its cost to the college and to the individuals, and the consequences the program will have for the image of the sponsoring institution. They deserve candid answers to these entirely pertinent questions.

They may also raise questions that seem somewhat less reasonable: "What do you intend to do about bathing?" "Wouldn't it be better to go to Belgium in view of the French trade discrimination against the United States?" "Can you really trust Spaniards?" Fortunately, we have passed through the era when that sort of conservatism was widespread; but it can still be found, and the trip organizer must be prepared to meet it with the same indulgence accorded to the more sophisticated questions.

One needs to pin down a list of exactly what the administration will require in order to approve the program, then work at satisfying these requirements. They will no doubt include a detailed itinerary, a description of the course work, an accurate statement of cost. The school attorney should look into the matters of liability and insurance. Considering the slowness of typical approval procedures and in view of the work this will entail for the program organizer, particularly when correspondence with foreign schools and travel services is envisioned, a period of six to nine months is not too long to allow for preparations of this type. Another semester or two will be required to recruit the students.

LOGISTICS

The program director will find that he
has enough to do just taking care of matters
on the American side: recruitment, orientation, correspondence, budget; he will be
wise to leave to other hands the task of
setting up the overseas arrangements:
lodging, meals, teachers, classrooms, transportation, guides. If the program is to be
basically an educational tour, the arrangements can be made through any reputable
agency with experience in student travel.
The cost is no higher when bookings are
made through an agent, whereas the convenience is considerable. If classroom space,
native teachers, dormitories, or private
homes are required, the matter had best be
turned over to a person (probably a teacher)
who lives in the town where the overseas
campus is to be located. This individual
would inspect the homes, interview prospective teachers, negotiate for classrooms and
dormitory space, and deal with the local
travel services. Naturally, this representative should be paid for his work.

There is little risk in accepting hotel,
restaurant, and motorcoach accommodations
that you are unable to check out in advance,
as these services are classified by the
respective ministries of tourism, and the
quality of each category is fairly consistent from town to town. In the case where
dormitory accommodations or private homes
are to be used, however, these must be
inspected by a person representing the U.S.
school who has the necessary contacts and
who understands precisely what the program
director expects. The same principle
applies if native instructors will be

employed. It would be virtually impossible
for the director to write to the dozens of
hotels, bus companies, and restaurants, even
if he knew the addresses. Hence, the
recommendation that an agent be retained.
When the tasks of recruiting a foreign staff
and visiting scores of homes are added, it
will be apparent why it is preferable to
engage someone in the country to look out for
the school's interests and to coordinate the
entire overseas operation, at least during
the organizational year. In normal circumstances, a period of several months would be
required to put the overseas portion together. Even if money and released time could
be found to permit the program director to
make an exploratory trip abroad, he would
have time to do no more than look over the
arrangements that the local representative
had already lined up.

KEEPING COSTS DOWN

   Offering a program that will attract
students while keeping the price low enough
so that they will not be frightened off is
a major problem confronting the organizer.
Fortunately, there are ways to trim costs.

   Air fare. The greatest single item in
the budget is of course transoceanic transportation; but charter flights and youth
fares will help keep this expenditure down.
The day has passed when the ship was cheaper
than the plane, for even scheduled flights
are now less costly than sailing, and
charters are cheaper yet. Passenger comfort
and inflight services on charter flights,
having made tremendous strides since the era
of the old "non-skeds," are now on a par

with those of the main international air-
lines. So air travel will no doubt be
chosen, unless -and this is a distinct
possibility- four to six days aboard an
ocean liner can be turned into a profitable
orientation period.

While it is difficult for the average
college to fill even the smallest charter
plane (167 seats), a number of student
travel organizations now sponsor charters
for which any college group can qualify.
If any but the best known lines are flown,
however, the inevitable questions should be
shortcircuited by making the company's
safety record part of the routine literature
for the program. The Civil Aeronautics
Board in Washington, D.C. can provide this
information. The records of charter
carriers are, incidentally, surprisingly
good.

Lodging. Hotels of higher than the two-
star category would be sheer extravagance
for our purposes. A quite satisfactory
formula for lodging student groups on tour
is the one-star hotel with three persons to
a room, and bath or shower shared between
two rooms. There would be hot and cold run-
ning water in all these "triples with fifty
percent bath," but some participants would
have to use the shower connected to the room
of another threesome in the group. This can
create certain inconveniences, to be sure;
but to move up to "doubles with one hundred
percent bath" would triple hotel costs. By
the way, it may take some searching to find
an innkeeper who is willing to accept a
group on the basis of triples with fifty
percent bath, and this is where a knowledgeable agent can be very helpful.

311

Lodging costs can be further reduced by using youth hostels where available. Availability, of course, is one of the major drawbacks, as there will not be a hostel everywhere the group is scheduled to go. On top of that, many hostels do not accept groups or they limit the size of groups to eight or ten members. Other hostels restrict one's sojourn to one or two days, and there are often age and membership requirements. Still others have obligatory work projects or early curfews that cut into valuable sightseeing time. Then hostels are sure to be packed during any school vacation period, and many are quite primitive. A number of new, modern youth hostels have sprung up recently in Western Europe, and in many hostels, old and new, a guest is as free to come and go as at an American YMCA. Given such variations, the program organizer will need to investigate all aspects of a youth hostel before writing that particular stop into the itinerary. The offices of American Youth Hostels in major U.S. cities can provide the details.

If students will be attending classes in one place for a week or more, lodging in dormitories or homes might be considered. Space in a boarding school or in university residence halls is not very difficult to arrange, especially if a representative on the spot is handling things, as has been suggested.

A home-stay is considerably more difficult to organize. First, just the task of finding several dozen families in the same town willing to lodge and feed a foreigner for a given period of time, probably during their own vacation, is difficult enough.

Later, conflicts arise -over the bathroom,
meals, personalities, curfew- necessitating
mediation on the part of the program director. Furthermore, communications between
the director and the group members become
extremely difficult when the students are
quartered all over town. All of this is
not to say that lodging in families cannot
be successful, but certainly the drawbacks
just mentioned should be weighed before
rejecting the uniformity and convenience of
dormitory living.

Whether lodging is in families or in
dormitories, a clear agreement is needed
between the parties as to what the accommodations will consist of and what the
institution's or family's responsibilities
are to be. Ideally, this would take the
form of a legal contract and would clarify
such details as laundry, bathroom, telephone,
and kitchen privileges, meal hours and menus,
the curfew if any, the dates of the sojourn,
the price of the accommodations, and the
settlement in case of cancellation. The
student, then, should be made fully aware of
all conditions and restrictions when he
signs up for the program.

Surface transportation. One normally
pays the same price to charter a motorcoach
for a dozen passengers as for three dozen.
This has important implications when economy
is essential, as the more unoccupied seats
there are, the higher the per-passenger cost.
It may be useful to think of the program's
enrollment capacity in terms of "bus-fuls".
As Europen touring coaches accommodate from
thirty-five to forty-five persons, a
chartered coach provides economical transportation for a group of thirty to forty-

313

five. If the group exceeds forty-five by
only a few and a second bus is hired, a
great number of empty seats will result and
the pro-rata cost will rise above what it
would have been had a ceiling of forty-five
participants been established. Naturally,
if two buses can be filled or nearly filled,
so much the better. If there are fewer than
twenty-five members in the group, rail transportation will prove more economical.

The great beauty of the motorcoach is
its flexibility. It can penetrate where
railroads and airports have never been
built, and it will stop when trains and
planes only whiz on by. The bus deserves
consideration, therefore, even when it is
not the most economical of either time or
money, and itineraries should be planned to
take advantage of its flexibility. Distance
and the condition of the roads become
secondary considerations. In the long run,
actual savings can often be realized by *not*
taking the most direct route. For example,
there is no need to pay for a special trip
to see Chartres, if you have already stopped
there en route from Paris to the Loire
Valley.

Meals. Breakfast is always included in
the price of the room in one- and two-star
European hotels. It would be advisable to
include one other meal per day in the price
of the program, in the interest of preventing illness. Normally, this would be the
evening meal. Lunch should be left open,
except when touring, so that the students
do not have to interrupt their activities
to return to the hotel to eat. When on
tour in remote or unfamiliar areas lunch
should be provided, so that time is not lost

314

searching around for a suitable restaurant.
About three dollars is trimmed from the
asking price of the program every time a
restaurant stop is eliminated. Naturally,
the cost of the lunch is still an expense
to the student; but the individual who will
settle for a snack at noon can save himself
a considerable amount of money if he is
left to his own devices for lunch.

   Discounts. The many discounts that a
student group can take advantage of, simply
because they are students and a group, may
be too numerous to detail here, but they
are so advantageous that they definitely
deserve the attention of the program
organizer. There are group theater rates,
university restaurants, free student admission to museums, even considerations in
shops. As a rule of thumb, one should *never*
buy entrance tickets of any kind, book
passage on any conveyance, or reserve any
sort of accommodations without first dicker-
ing for a group rate. This largely Old World
practice makes many Americans uneasy. There
is no need to feel this way. It is usually
enough to declare that one is the leader of
a school group -at national monuments, it is
best to have an attestation from the
ministry of education- and the discount is
unquestioningly accorded. The most embarrassing reply one can receive is, "That *is*
the group rate." In tourist-class hotels,
one room per fifteen or twenty persons is
routinely complimented. On European railroads, the reduction can be as high as forty
percent.

   It may seem of small consequence to trim
five dollars, let us say, from the price of
a railroad ticket, but considering it in

terms of the savings for the budget as a
whole gives quite another perspective. This
five dollar saving multiplied by the forty
participants we hope to have in our group
equals two hundred dollars--that is, one-
fifth of one student's trip fees, on the
average. And the same surprising multipli-
cation takes place every time the group
enters a museum, has a meal, or checks into
a hotel.

   Funding. It would be unrealistic, in
this day of financial cutbacks, to *count on*
funding from the school. Avenues for obtaining funds should, nonetheless, be explored,
as an occasional scholarship or grant for
curriculum development is still available.
The sponsoring institution should at least
be persuaded to pick up office and printing
expenses and the salary of the program
director.

   Foreign Study in the Western Hemisphere.
French and Spanish program planners have
alternatives that their colleagues in other
languages do not have: the linguistically
foreign cultures in North and South America.
Whether preference or financial considerations prompt the choice of Latin America or
Quebec, most of what we have said in speaking of Europe will also apply.

ESTABLISHING THE BUDGET

   One of the first steps in organizing a
travel program is to draw up a dependable
breakdown of all costs, the obvious ones
(transportation, lodging, board, tuition,
salaries, printing, office expenses, the
director's trip) and the ones we might tend
to overlook (tips, insurance, gifts,

316

entertainment, airport taxes, and inflation). There is no room for guess-work
here. Care should be taken to project as
accurately as possible every conceivable
outlay before announcing the program and
its price. For if it is discovered after
the students have signed up that the fees
do not cover program costs, only two solutions are open: a cutback in the program
or the addition of a surcharge. Either of
these would seriously undermine confidence
in the program.

Inflation. Inflation has been increasing European travel costs at an average
rate of three per cent a year since 1965.
Fluctuations in foreign exchange rates can
also add considerably to financial problems.
There is no sure formula, but it is certain
that an allowance for rises in costs should
be made.

Tips. It should be clearly understood
whether tips for chambermaids, drivers,
porters, waiters, and guides have been
included in the quotations furnished by the
contractors. Even if the gratuity has been
included, will the personnel still expect
something on the side? That question must
be asked point-blank of the travel agent.

Gifts and entertainment. Beyond the
Anglo-Saxon community, the wheels of business relations are kept turning, it would
seem, by cups of coffee, bottles of wine,
boxes of chocolates, and countless other
little gifts and generosities. This is
particularly true if the facilities of
foreign campuses or homes are used. Perhaps
even a dinner or a reception will be in
order. The persons exercising budgetary

317

control must recognize these items as legitimate operating expenses.

Liability Insurance. The school attorney should look thoroughly into the matter of liability and recommend an insurance program. He will surely conclude that a good liability insurance policy, backed up with a well-worded release form, is indispensable. The price of the program must reflect these insurance costs.

BAGGAGE AND MEDICAL INSURANCE

It is not practical for the school to sponsor a group insurance program. Most of the students will find that they are already covered, by the family's health and accident insurance for medical expenses and by their parents' householder's policy for baggage insurance. In the rare instances where this is not the case, the student would do far better to deal with an insurance agent on an individual basis, as the premium for a group policy for the handful of exceptions would prove far too costly. Naturally, the group insurance could be made compulsory, but that would seem a pointless duplication where existing insurance is adequate. The students or their parents should definitely check with their agent to see that coverage does in fact apply for the countries concerned, as some insurance has geographical restrictions.

THE CAMPUS, THE COURSES, AND THE ITINERARY

Where the group will go, what they will see, and what they will study are determined by the students' background and goals, the organizer's expectations, and the limitations of time and money. The most we can do here is to give a few guidelines.

If the program is basically an educational tour, the participants should have some background in the history, architecture, art, geography, literature and sociological aspects of the places they will visit. Whether the itinerary is dictated by courses already existing or whether special orientation courses are to be developed must be decided by the school for itself.

If classroom attendance will play a part in the program, we should keep in mind that one learns best what he can put immediately into practice. Language classes should, therefore, concentrate on conversational situations that the students will readily encounter, and much of the time scheduled for cultural courses should be devoted to acquiring background for the field trips.

If a language program is the basic aim, the campus should be located in a spot where the opportunity to speak English is minimal. Unfortunately, this criterion categorically eliminates Paris, Rome, Athens, and most major German cities. Yet, although the capitals (except Madrid and Lisbon) are out, we must still find a place where entertainment and recreational facilities are available. The town that "rolls up the sidewalks" at ten is not conducive to good group morale; moreover, it provides far fewer opportunities to mix with the local people. There should be cinemas, sports, museums, interesting cafés, and active clubs. There should also be opportunities for excursions into the countryside: castles, woods, beaches, islands, picturesque towns, historical sites. And there should be a good proportion of young people in the population.

During the spring and summer, resort areas that attract relatively few English-speaking tourists come closest to fulfilling these ideals. Examples are few, and the supply is diminishing. At the risk of becoming dated very quickly, let us suggest the Breton seaside towns, the southern Adriatic shores of Italy, and the spas and beaches of Lower Saxony. While prejudice against the idiom of these areas might have made us hesitate to recommend them a genera-tion ago, in this day of mass media one can count on all but the most backwoods inhabi-tants setting a worthy example for the foreign language student!

If classrooms are required, we are further limited to a town with a university or high school. In the long run, it will probably prove preferable to enroll the students in an already established summer school in a town that more or less meets our requirements, rather than develop a program from the ground up. A directory of such schools can be obtained from the respective foreign consulates, and the consul or cultural attaché himself will no doubt be pleased to act as a go-between. If the group is large enough, he may be able to arrange specially tailored courses. Using an established summer school will not only entail much less work than setting up a new program, it will no doubt be less costly as well.

GUIDED TOURS

   Scorn is frequently heaped upon group
touring, especially that of the "If-this-is
Tuesday-this-must-be-Belgium" variety. Let
us consider, however, the prospect of completely unstructured sightseeing: the students arrive in a strange town, lose a
great deal of time just finding out what
there is to see, waste more time experimenting with public transportation, end up spending money on cabs, use valuable minutes
standing in line for tickets, and finally
only half-understand the little they have
time left to look at. No wonder that after
a few discouraging days like this they
prefer to stay in their rooms and "rap"
-usually negatively- about the trip!

   A touring coach with a professional
guide eliminates this waste, provides a
meaningful visit, and furnishes excellent
orientation for in-depth enjoyment on an
individual basis later during the free time.
It is important that the guide be told that
the students have already studied the places
to which he is taking them, and that they
will be returning later that day or later in
the week. Typically, the guide will be
pleased to know that he has such a receptive
audience; he will put more into it than he
does for the housewives from Topeka, and in
the process he will stir up just the sort of
enthusiasm for these return visits that we
want the student to have.

   It should be understood that such orientation tours are by nature cursory and somewhat rushed. They do provide background for,
but they do not replace, the more leisurely
return visits for which time has built into

the program. To make the introductory tour as efficient as possible, all participants must cooperate by keeping up with the group, being attentive to the guide, not stopping to buy things, and returning to the bus on time. These responsibilities toward the other group members should be impressed on the students during the orientation sessions.

Certainly, a half-day of guided sightseeing in any major city would not be too much. Rome, in fact deserves at least two half-days. In most cities, a half-day would give only time enough to see where the major landmarks are located and how to reach them on public transportation. There would not be time to go inside.

Whether guided visits of the interiors are added will depend on the particular interests of the group; and whether a special guide is hired will depend on the capabilities of the program staff and on the strength of the local guide union. A teacher is always permitted to serve as guide to his own students aboard the motor-coaches and in the street, but in most areas it will be obligatory to engage an official guide when a commented visit is desired in museums, cathedrals, galleries, castles, and their grounds. Before the program director addresses his students as a group in such places, he should inquire about the policy, for otherwise he risks an embarrassing reprimand from the guard or a union representative. Any tour agency in Europe can provide an expert guide, licensed by the ministry of tourism. The cost of the guide is included with the entrance ticket in some places, particularly castles and historic homes.

PEOPLE TO PEOPLE

Social events, recreation, and sports
are essential outlets and morale builders,
and they deserve a place in our program if
for those reasons alone. Their function is,
moreover, educative; for what is a volley-
ball game for a language student if all his
teammates are Italian, but one of the very
best Italian lessons he could hope for?

The students want desperately to meet
and talk with their foreign counterparts.
They most often give as their major reason
for enrolling in the program their desire
to improve their oral facility in the language and their understanding of the people.
Yet we hear many programs criticized for
their failure to provide opportunities for
"practicing on the natives." There they are
surrounded by native-speakers, yet their big
day was the one when they bought a chocolate
eclair "all in French." Or they traveled
all the way to Salzburg, only to spend the
summer speaking pidgin-German *to each other*!
The problem is that the program's planners
felt it was sufficient to lead the horse to
water. Obviously, even complete submersion
was not enough!

In view of the structure and span of the
short-term group trip, international inter-
personal contacts need to be planned as
carefully as the itinerary and the classroom
instruction. And let us not forget that a
twenty-year-old's idea of "meeting the
people" is not to shake hands in a reception
line with the mayor of Salamanca. A thrill-
ing moment, perhaps, especially in the
retelling, but hardly the linguistic and
social experience the young American needs

323

and craves: the companionship of Spaniards his own age, sipping *tinto* in some student hangout, and singing folksongs till three to the accompaniment of a guitar passed round the circle.

Such contacts, even deep, lasting friendships, can be developed; but they are not usually spontaneous--that is, let us reiterate, in the context of the organized program of short duration. The Americans live together, they eat together, and they attend classes together. They all get aboard a bus and go off sightseeing. Then they wonder why it is so hard to meet the natives! Ironically enough, these same natives are at the same time asking themselves why the Americans are so aloof and cliquish.

Preventing such a situation requires of the program director an active nurturing of social contacts for his students and on the part of the students a consciously open frame of mind. They must understand that if they wait for the local people to seek them out, they may wait forever. While a foreigner on a small U.S. campus is still a novelty, the European at least has grown blase about Americans--if he is not actually put off by us. Our bare feet, our energetic gum-chewing techniques, the piercing squeals with which we punctuate our conversation may be accepted form on Main Street, but they shock on Friedrichstrasse. We do not ask our young Americans to stop being young or Americans, but they do have to understand that they must blend in to be accepted, especially in the provincial town where we hope our campus will be located. Then they must resign themselves to shunning

the company of other Americans for awhile,
and plunge instead into activities that will
put them in touch with the local young
people. The students can make acquaintances
with ease by enrolling in a sailing school,
by joining a mountain-climbing club, by
talking with fellow weight-lifters at the
gym, or by cultivating an interest in a
folklore society or camera club.

The role of the program director in all
this is to seek out places where young
people congregate. A call at the neighborhood rectory should provide information on
the local youth organizations. Their members can then be invited to songfests and
bike hikes. They (and their brothers,
sisters, cousins, and friends) can fill up
the empty seats on the excursion buses.
This may entail furnishing a few extra box
lunches, but the expense is certainly
justifiable, as the gesture will pay off in
the form of multiplied and mutually gratify-
ing contacts. One test for the effectiveness
of the entire foreign study program now
suggests itself: a comparison of the students' ability to use the familiar form of
address conversationally before and after
the trip.

ORIENTATION

A reading list should be drawn up to
provide background in cuisine, history, art,
architecture, government, economics. These
topics then need to be discussed in orientation sessions prior to departure, whether a
specific orientation period is set up or,
rather, one or more semester-long orientation courses are instituted as part of the
curriculum. This information is needed from

the moment of arrival, so it would be too late to do it justice once the trip has begun. Besides, the time overseas is just too brief and too costly to spend acquiring background that can be got at home.

In addition to information that can readily be found in books, the teacher should not overlook attitudes and folkways-- the Spanish pride, German door protocol, the French mania for switching off lights, Italian flirtation techniques (as a defensive measure). These are serious matters, as understanding them will add to the students' appreciation, and spare them embarrassing gaffs. The simple knowledge that the train conductor will not be at all interested in your ticket *during* the trip, but that you must turn in the ticket to get out of the station will prove tremendously useful, for example.

Also part of the orientation process is the distribution of a clothing list and instructions for procuring travel documents. As students are frequently hostile to anything an authority figure has to say about their dress, the clothing list would be more readily acceptable if it were drawn up by the students themselves on the basis of discussions with fellow-students and young faculty members who have recently returned from abroad. A student who can relate how he got chased home by a gang of ruffians in Madrid the day he wore his white jeans will be a thousand times more convincing than an hour of harangue from an older person. The same technique might be used to make the reading list more palatable.

The orientation is also a time to get

organized for travel as a group. Much time and energy can be saved if everyone knows what to expect, step by step, in airports, at customs, in hotels. One should not wait until a couple of late-risers have kept a bus full of people waiting to deliver a tirade on punctuality. It is during the orientation that understandings should be reached on such individual responsibilities to the other members of the group.

CONDITIONS

When the program is finally announced, all conditions should be stated definitively and in writing, to avoid room for complaint later. The price of the program and what this fee includes and does not include, any standards of conduct that will be enforced, who can be accepted into the program and on what conditions one can be separated from it (illness, behavior, personal convenience), the refund policy in every case--all these matters should be clearly spelled out and understood by all. One should in fact be quite specific: which meals are included and which are at the expense of the student? How many baths are allowed per week where the student will be living? An accurate estimate of essential pocket money should be given, with a listing of what it will cover and will not cover. Here as everywhere, the credibility gap must be kept minimal. Deadlines and payment schedules should be set, and the schedule of orientation sessions published. Some sort of agreement of participation, a form setting forth program conditions and signed by the student, is in fact desirable.

THE PROGRAM DIRECTOR

This discussion has revealed the versatility required of the person chosen to organize and direct such a program. He must be a teacher, an administrator, an expert in matters of tourism, a big brother, a disciplinarian, a counselor, an interpreter, a businessman, and a diplomat. We sometimes hear laymen express astonishment that the program director "gets his trip free." There is nothing *free* about it. He is chained to the responsibility twenty-four hours a day, and his work-day can run to ten or twelve hours, for when he is not actually conducting tours, briefings, or counseling sessions, he is on the telephone or out in town setting up social contacts, planning activities, ironing out logistical kinks. When illness, unfavorable weather, or hotel cancellations strike, his work can easily be doubled.

When a director-to-be begins to inquire about how much free time he will have, whether he will have any evening duty (when will he not?), whether he can schedule a few days to visit his cousin in Essex, then we can be sure he has not grasped what it means to be a foreign program director, and we should seriously doubt his chances of being a success at the job. The position demands a person fully dedicated to the program, who will not object to long hours, who can get along in close contact with the same people for an extended period, who has ingenuity, adaptability, and originality, who has stamina, who is an imperturbable traveler, and who will do everything he can to see that all students reap the maximum advantage from the travel experience. Anyone looking for a free ride need not apply.

34. COMMUNITY COLLEGE PROGRAMS: A REPORT OF A CONFERENCE IN WASHINGTON STATE

SUSAN E. KARR
University of Washington

During the Illinois Conference on Foreign Languages in Junior and Community Colleges held in March, 1972 the suggestion was made that junior college teacher training programs should focus on those already teaching at the two-year level. In an attempt to implement this suggestion locally, a two-day workshop was held May 26-27 for Washington's community college foreign language teachers.

The purpose of the workshop -sponsored by a Kellogg grant made available through the University of Washington's Center for the Development of Community College Education- was to provide a forum for the community college foreign language teachers from around the state, who almost without exception are facing the problem of declining enrollments. Mr. Keith D. Crosbie, State Supervisor of Foreign Language Programs,

Ms. Susan E. Karr, doctoral candidate in German at the University of Washington, and Mr. Leon Appelbaum, instructor of German and French at North Seattle Community College, organized the workshop, which was attended by 25 teachers, or approximately 33% of all full-time community college foreign language teachers in Washington.

Much of the first day of the workshop was devoted to outlining and establishing priorities for the problems which face Washington's foreign language teachers at the community college level. Dr. Henry Cordes, Chairman of the Foreign Language Department at the College of San Mateo, California, who was a visiting consultant at the conference, opened the meeting with a discussion of problems which teachers face at his institution and of ways his college, and specifically his department, have moved to counter the apparently nation-wide trend of declining foreign language enrollments. Major complaints by local teachers included the low priority usually given foreign language study when budgets are determined, students' attitudes towards the study of a foreign language, and the lack of articulation between high schools, community colleges, and four-year institutions.

During the second day of the workshop the teachers heard a talk on the individualization of foreign language instruction given by Dr. Howard B. Altman, Assistant Professor of German at the University of Washington. They then spent several hours discussing possible solutions to the problems which face them. Suggestions for ways to improve offerings and raise enrollments included introducing experimental courses

in both English and the various languages,
substituting meaningful individual projects
for traditional final exams, and finding ways
of attracting advanced high school students
into the college's programs. There was also
discussion of the feasibility of offering 10
or even 15 credit hour intensive courses during the Spring and/or Summer Quarters. Other
suggestions included introducing new approaches to testing, recruiting advanced students to serve as aides in beginning classes,
offering beginning courses in both Autumn and
Winter Quarters, and scheduling conversation
courses during the summer for high school
students with one to four years of background
in a given language.

In addition to discussing ways to improve
their own courses, teachers also considered
methods of involving others in the drive to
increase enrollments. One teacher suggested
that people in the community should be encouraged to offer prizes to outstanding students, while another urged teachers to talk
with the teachers of vocational and occupa-
tional courses; the latter teacher stated
that at his school those students working
towards certification as ski school instructors now have the option of taking some
basic French. Several teachers suggested the
establishment of adequate resource centers
with language laboratories and available
tutors, and one pressed for the development
of a central clearinghouse in the state for
storage of audio-visual aids, including
films. Additional suggestions included ways
to attract federal cooperative funding programs into the language areas, demanding a
greater voice in the colleges' budgetary
allocations, and submitting a comprehensive

proposal for the state-wide development of
foreign language programs to the Washington
Instructional Council.

ILLINOIS CONFERENCE ON FOREIGN LANGUAGES IN JUNIOR AND COMMUNITY COLLEGES

Champaign, March 23-25, 1972

PARTICIPANTS

Louise H. Allen
Parkland College
Champaign, Ill.

Howard B. Altman
Department of German
University of Washington
Seattle, Wash.

Ray Archer
Prairie State College
Chicago Heights, Ill.

Bill Berman
Houghton-Mifflin Co.
Boston, Mass.

Grace M. Brashier
Belleville Area College
Belleville, Ill.

D. Lincoln Canfield
Southern Illinois University
Carbondale, Ill.

Gerald F. Carr
Eastern Illinois University
Charleston, Ill.

Gloria Dowling
Department of ESL
University of Illinois
Urbana, Ill.

C. L. Dawson
Department of Slavic Languages
University of Illinois
Urbana, Ill.

Vincent J. Dell'Orto
Department of German
University of Illinois
Urbana, Ill.

Jimmie Deones
Olney Central College
Olney, Ill.

H. Michael Dunn
Department of Classics
University of Illinois
Urbana, Ill.

Lorel Beth Ellsworth
Department of French
University of Illinois
Urbana, Ill.

Merle Ferris
Department of ESL
University of Illinois
Urbana, Ill.

Richard C. Figge
Department of German
University of Illinois
Urbana, Ill.

Rita Flaherty
Triton Community College
River Grove, Ill.

Joseph S. Flores
Department of Spanish
University of Illinois
Urbana, Ill.

Nyla Gilkerson
Waubonsee Community College
Sugar Grove, Ill.

Lee E. Hawkins
Department of Secondary and
    Continuing Education
University of Illinois
Urbana, Ill.

David Herschberg
Department of Spanish
University of Illinois
Urbana, Ill.

Ruth Holland
Wabash Valley College
Mt. Carmel, Ill.

Walter F. Holland
Wabash Valley College
Mt. Carmel, Ill.

Susan E. Karr
Department of German
University of Washington
Seattle, Wash.

Kurt Klein
Department of Slavic Languages
University of Illinois
Urbana, Ill.

Bruce Mainous
Department of French
University of Illinois
Urbana, Ill.

Sister Marie Celeste
Office of Superintendent of Public
    Instruction
Springfield, Ill.

Hilda Markowski
Triton Community College
River Grove, Ill.

Vivian Masters
Illinois Central College
East Peoria, Ill.

Frederick W. Murray
Department of Foreign Languages
Northern Illinois University
DeKalb, Ill.

Dan O'Rourke
Prairie State College
Chicago Heights, Ill.

Monika Patel
Oakton Community College
Morton Grove, Ill.

Guenter Pfister
Southern Illinois University
Carbondale, Ill.

Aurora Quirós de Haggard
Loop College
Chicago, Ill.

Barbara Raither
Danville Junior College
Danville, Ill.

Georgia Reed
Danville Junior College
Danville, Ill.

Wilga Rivers
Department of French
University of Illinois
Urbana, Ill.

Peter Russo
College of DuPage
Glen Ellyn, Ill.

Jon Mason Sams
Shawnee Community College
Ullin, Ill.

Sandra Savignon
Department of French
University of Illinois
Urbana, Ill.

Richard Scanlan
Department of Classics
University of Illinois
Urbana, Ill.

Susanna Schuler
Illinois Central College
East Peoria, Ill.

Pamela C. Strange
Danville Junior College
Danville, Ill.

Kenneth Strickler
Parkland College
Champaign, Ill.

Carmen Upchurch
Elgin Community College
Elgin, Ill.

Shirley Verdugo-Perez
Department of Spanish, Italian, and
    Portuguese
University of Illinois at Chicago Circle
Chicago, Ill.

Elizabeth Wachs
Parkland College
Champaign, Ill.

Don E. Wood
Seminole Junior College
Seminole, Okla.

PARTICIPANTS
PREPARATORY REGIONAL CONFERENCES IN ILLINOIS

January, 1972

CHAMPAIGN REGIONAL CONFERENCE

Coordinator: Louise H. Allen
Parkland College
Champaign, Illinois

Parkland College
Danute Reisner
Kenneth Strickler
Kaethe P. Wilber

*Illinois State
University*
A. Gordon Ferguson
Robert Roussey

University of Illinois
W. Curtis Blaylock
Clayton Dawson
Vincent Dell'Orto
H. Michael Dunn
Joseph S. Flores
Richard Figge

Rend Lake College
Carol A. DeSelms

*Eastern Illinois
University*
Paul Kirby
Martin Miess

David Hershberg
Kurt A. Klein
Robert J. Nelson
Wilga M. Rivers
Sandra J. Savignon

SPRINGFIELD REGIONAL CONFERENCE

Coordinator: Vivian Masters
Illinois Central College
East Peoria, Illinois

Carl Sandburg College
Marwan Nahas

Illinois Central College
Tony Alle
Joseph James
Charles Wright

Illinois Valley Community College
Kathryn Lillyman

UPSTATE NORTH REGIONAL CONFERENCE

Coordinator: Nyla Gilkerson
Waubonsee Community College
Sugar Grove, Illinois

Kishwaukee College
Robert Jones

Waubonsee Community College
Denise Bouchet

Northern Illinois University
Raimo Itkonen

Rock Valley College
Donald Smith

340